NEW WORK SCHEDULES
FOR
A CHANGING SOCIETY

A Work in America Institute
Policy Study

Directed by Jerome M. Rosow, President,
and Robert Zager, Vice-President
for Policy Studies and Technical Assistance

Work in America Institute, Inc., Scarsdale, New York

CHICAGO RESEARCH AND TRADING GROUP, LTD.
440 SOUTH LA SALLE STREET
CHICAGO, ILLINOIS 60605

9/14/87
DW

The material for the publications produced as part of this project was prepared under grant number 80-19 of The Commonwealth Fund and under a grant from the Carnegie Corporation of New York.

Library of Congress Catalog Card No. 81-7583
ISBN No. 0-89361-025-9

Printed in the United States of America

Library of Congress Cataloging in Publication Data

Work in America Institute.
New work schedules for a changing society.

Includes bibliographical references.
1. Hours of labor—United States. 2. Hours of labor, Flexible—United States. 3. Four-day week—United States. 4. Part-time employment—United States. I. Title.
HD5124.W6   1981   658.3'121'0973   81-7583
ISBN 0-89361-025-9   AACR2

This report can be ordered from the Publications Department, Work in America Institute, Inc., 700 White Plains Road, Scarsdale, New York 10583. Please allow 4-6 weeks for delivery.

April 30, 1981

LETTER FROM THE BOARD OF DIRECTORS
WORK IN AMERICA INSTITUTE

New Work Schedules for a Changing Society and its companion casebook, *New Work Schedules in Practice*, bring home more dramatically than ever how far the U.S. has come, and how far it still must go, in freeing itself from the tyranny of the time clock.

For 150 years American employers and employees took it for granted that universal subjection to the clock was the price of efficiency. Only recently have employers begun to adopt new concepts of time management which consider it feasible to have efficiency *without* the lockstep. Ironically, we must all thank West Germany, so long identified with bureaucracy, for introducing the simple device—flexitime—that started the unfreezing of uniform work schedules.

Flexitime was invented not just to make life more pleasant for workers, but to solve a practical, immediate problem that beset a company and its employees together: traffic was blocking the firm's employees from getting to work on time, and operations were suffering as a result. It is also significant that a woman came up with the invention.

The unprecedented, unpredicted influx of women (especially mothers with school-age children) into paid employment highlighted the demographic, social, and economic changes that transformed the workplace in the 1970s. New family structures, new employee expectations, new demands for leisure and further education, rapid inflation, and geographic dispersal of plants and residences all combined to force employers to think about new ways of managing organizational time. New work schedules evolved as means of achieving a more reasonable balance between the competing demands of work, family, and personal life. This national policy study analyzes five major forms of new work schedules or job redesign which have great potential for the 1980s:

Flexitime
Permanent Part-Time Jobs
Shared Jobs
Compressed Workweeks
Work Sharing.

These five basic forms have been combined in new and novel ways so that the advantages of more than one pattern can be molded or redesigned to the needs of the work force and the organization. Flexitime has been combined with shorter workweeks. Part-time jobs have been translated into job sharing. Full-time jobs have been divided into shared jobs. Compressed weeks have emerged as an antidote to the growing resistance to shift work. And compressed weeks have defused the issue of involuntary overtime, especially Saturday and Sunday work.

All the new schedules offer certain advantages in common. They cost little or nothing to install; they require no changes in technology or plant; they require no organizational restructuring; and they help to improve productivity.

We endorse *New Work Schedules for a Changing Society* because, like the previous policy reports of Work in America Institute, it (1) deals with work innovations that benefit employers, employees, unions, and the general public, (2) focuses on the policy issues, the basic interests of the people involved, (3) clarifies the choices for decision makers, and (4) makes practical recommendations for those who want to progress in this area.

This report is remarkable because it comes to grips with a seminal change. Organizational behavior is responding to human needs in a form of accommodation which is mutually advantageous. We urge employers to take a fresh look at the conditions of work and the labor market and discover that the new options for time management are opportunities not to be missed.

Sincerely,

Work in America Institute, Inc.
Board of Directors

Ronald H. Brown

Irving Bluestone

H. W. Clarke, Jr.

Emilio G. Collado

Thomas R. Donahue

Clark Kerr

G.G. Michelson

Elliot L. Richardson

Jerome M. Rosow

Daniel Yankelovich

Contents

Preface

New Work Schedules for a Changing Society is the report of the third national policy study by Work in America Institute. Like its two predecessors, it bears the endorsement of the Institute's tripartite board of directors, reflecting the report's responsiveness to the mutual interests of labor, management, and the general public.

Each of our policy studies, including the present one, considers a subject of growing importance to the workplace during the coming decade. The objective of each is not to lay out alternatives or advocate ideal solutions, but to recommend practical courses of action, based on the "state of the art" and tested against the experience of knowledgeable leaders. It is an approach that should help decision makers in all types of organizations to act with enlightened self-interest.

New work schedules in the United States, after a slow start in the 1970s, have been expanding rapidly. We expect this upswing to continue throughout the 1980s because life-styles and family structures are changing and because employers and communities which respond creatively to the new conditions will gain a competitive edge. Look to the eighties, then, as the decade in which work schedules will undergo a major and lasting change.

This report is designed to guide employers in forming useful judgments about the policy issues involved in choosing, planning, and managing new work schedules. A companion volume, *New Work Schedules in Practice*, which is being published simultaneously by Van Nostrand Reinhold in the ongoing Van Nostrand Reinhold/Work in America Institute Series, illustrates the resolution of sticky issues by means of over 40 case studies of actual programs in the United States and Europe.

For their invaluable assistance in carrying out this project, we wish to express our thanks to the following:

The Commonwealth Fund and the Carnegie Corporation of New York, for financial support, encouragement, and commitment.

Our National Advisory Committee (whose names are listed on the inside of the front cover) for their no-holds-barred advice, their insights, and their active involvement in the policy process.

Professor Stanley D. Nollen, School of Business Administration, Georgetown University, and associate director of this study, for preparing many of the original drafts for chapters of the report (although he bears no responsibility for the end product).

Linda A. Ittner, for two discussion papers: "Part-Time Work," and "Work Sharing with Short-Time Compensation."

Gretl S. Meier, for her discussion paper on "Job Sharing."

Richard M. Prosten, for his discussion paper on "Union Attitudes toward New Work Schedules."

Frank W. Schiff, for his article on "Flexiplace."

Professor Richard W. Winett, for his discussion paper on the "Family Impact of New Work Schedules," and for his help in drafting part of the chapter on energy.

We particularly acknowledge the outstanding contribution of Robert Zager, who, as Work in America Institute's vice-president for policy studies, determined the parameters of the study, presided over advisory committee meetings with unfailing patience and good humor, and skillfully combined various viewpoints in a report that charts a new course for new work schedules in the 1980s.

We also acknowledge the skillful and dedicated contributions of other members of the Work in America Institute staff:

Joyce Derian, who coordinated the editing and production of the report.

Beatrice Walfish, who edited the manuscript.

Frances Harte, who supervised the production of the report and also designed its format, including the cover.

Joan White, who typeset and proofread the printed report, with the assistance of Stephanie McDowell.

Virginia Lentini, who managed the logistics of the entire study.

JEROME M. ROSOW
President
Work in America Institute, Inc.

September 1981

NEW WORK SCHEDULES
FOR
A CHANGING SOCIETY

Summary/
Recommendations

Ten years ago, new work schedules were a German import—foreign, different, and of unproven value. Today, 9.5 million full-time workers in the United States enjoy flexible work schedules and compressed workweeks, and an additional 11.8 million workers hold voluntary, permanent part-time jobs.

With more than one-fifth of the labor force now functioning under flexible, compressed, or voluntarily reduced work schedules, employers have literally tossed out time clocks, shredded time cards, and taken a new look at the nine-to-five day and the five-day week.

Strangely enough, the effect is not anarchy, or even a reduction of employee discipline, but rather increased self-management of time by workers and a new-found harmony between life-styles and work. The work ethic has been strengthened by reducing the stresses caused by the conflict between job demands, family needs, leisure values, and educational needs. And the accommodation of workplace demands to labor-market realities has been facilitated, with benefits accruing to both employers and employees.

New Work Schedules

How have work schedules changed?
- [ ] The *workday* has been shortened, lengthened, made both flexible and variable.
- [ ] The *workweek* has been compressed to two days, three days, four days, alternating three and four days, four and one-half days, and part-time weeks.
- [ ] The *workyear* has been reduced by longer blocks of leisure time—three-day and four-day holiday weekends, sabbaticals, furloughs (optional), and phased retirement to accommodate workers.

☐ *Flexitime* has been combined with compressed, shorter weeks. Part-time jobs have been linked to job sharing; job sharing has been linked to work sharing.

New work schedules have rapidly evolved into a wide variety of patterns, with the options many and still growing. They reflect the capacity and inventiveness of an open, democratic society that is ready to permit employees to take full responsibility for their attendance and performance at work without undue surveillance, controls, and restrictions.

Already the movement to build new work alternatives has resulted in the creation of unique new work schedules—flexitour, gliding time, maxiflex, and flexiplace—concepts unknown in the business world until several years ago. Through combinations and permutations, these new schedules reveal a new versatility and widening applicability, with all sectors of the economy, all industries, and all occupations open to change. The potential for reshaping and redesigning them into exciting new combinations is limited only by the imagination of people in work institutions.

Forecast for the 1980s

Work in America Institute predicts that the 1980s will witness far-reaching changes in work schedules to meet the needs of this changing society. We believe that by 1990:

☐ Twenty-five percent of full-time nonagricultural workers in the United States will be on flexible work schedules, 5 percent will have compressed workweeks, and 28 percent will be engaged in part-time work, job sharing, and work sharing.

☐ The workweek will be reduced to 36 hours, with new options for the nine-hour day, four-day week, as a pattern to eventually replace the eight-hour day, five-day week.

☐ Employers will recognize the economic advantages and social benefits of new work schedules as a fast-track method of meeting employee demands for better quality of working life.

☐ Work sharing will emerge as an intelligent alternative to layoffs and unemployment.

Social Trends

Work in America Institute believes that during the decade ahead certain social and demographic trends will provide an almost irresistible force, pushing employers in the direction of further experimentation with new work schedules. These trends will include:

☐ Multiple-worker and dual-career families.

☐ A continued increase in the participation rate of women in the work force.

☐ Increased capital-cost pressures to use shift work and overtime.

☐ Increased preference of workers to trade money for time off.

    ☐ Increased difficulty and cost of commutation.

    ☐ Broader dissemination of innovative work schedules, with employers spurred on by economic incentives.

    ☐ The desire of employees to participate in decisions on the scheduling of work time.

    ☐ The ability of semiautonomous work groups, teams, and individuals to relieve management of controversial or troublesome scheduling problems by self-managed choices, bargaining, and group decisions.

National Goals

The changes in work scheduling that have taken place during the last decade have substantially increased employee choices over their personal and professional lives. But work scheduling is more than a purely social issue; flexible work schedules can help further national goals, particularly in energy conservation and productivity growth. Compressed workweeks, for example, can substantially cut energy consumption. Flexible schedules of all kinds can raise morale and boost productivity. And work sharing, which avoids layoffs by distributing reduced work time among all of a plant's employees, can serve as a cushion against cyclical recessions.

Yet in order to achieve those goals, flexible work schedules must be chosen and implemented carefully. Employers must choose from a myriad of different flexible scheduling programs, not all of which are suitable for every workplace. New scheduling efforts may encounter stiff union resistance because of their potential for conflict with existing overtime laws. And any plan selected must be supported by first-line supervisors and nurtured through its early phases by careful cooperation between employees and management.

The single most important obstacle to new work schedules is still the autocratic tradition of supervision, founded on the belief, deeply imbedded by custom and practice, that rigid work schedules are essential to efficiency. It is imperative, then, that supervisors who are out of step with society be reoriented to understand the goals of new work schedules and to undertake a higher level of responsibility than that required by timekeeping.

Work in America Institute Policy Study

In order to document experiments with flexible work schedules, determine their successes and failures, and present recommendations to aid future alternative work schedule projects, the Work in America Institute embarked in 1979 on an eighteen-month policy study funded by The Commonwealth Fund and the Carnegie Corporation of New York. *New Work Schedules for a Changing Society*, the report resulting from this study, emphasizes policy issues and recommendations and is one of two books produced under the grant. The other, *New Work Schedules in Practice*, by Stanley Nollen, associate director of the policy study, concentrates on actual case descriptions to illustrate major policy issues and their solutions.

New Work Schedules for a Changing Society is divided into three major sections, "Time Management in the 1980s," "Policy Issues Inside the Organization," and "Broader Policy Issues." The first section discusses the economic and social setting for debate on new schedules, the varieties of schedules in use, and their advantages and disadvantages. The second section offers practical advice to employers and unions on steps to determine whether a new schedule is desirable, whether it will succeed, which type of new schedule to implement, and how to make the operation of new work schedules successful. The third section discusses the implications of new work schedules for broad social issues—transportation and energy policy, family and personal life, national employment policy, and labor relations.

Conclusions of the Study

The study has reached several broad conclusions of interest to employers, labor unions, and individual employees who would like to adopt alternative work schedules:

- The repackaging of work schedules will be increasingly necessary as a means of meeting the demands of the changing work force of the 1980s. More and more, the initiative for new work schedules comes from the work force rather than from management.
- New work schedules are win/win situations for employers and employees. Employers notice productivity improvements reflected by fewer paid absences and idle time, improved organization of work over the day, accommodation to the biological clocks of workers, and higher morale. Other gains are easier recruiting, less overtime pay, better use of production facilities, and opportunities to extend customer service. Yet new work schedules require no changes in work processes or technology; they require little or no capital investment.
- The quality-of-working-life agenda of the 1980s is inseparable from the redesign of work schedules. Many organizations have found that the most effective method for changing work schedules is to involve the workers themselves and their unions in planning, designing, and implementing them. In addition, flexitime and other work schedules, when successful, encourage employers to expand the range of decisions workers are free to make in other areas.
- The new variations of part-time employment which have emerged—job sharing, work sharing, temporary part-time employment, phased retirement, optional furloughs, and workyear contracts—

have introduced two key variables into work practice: permanence and choice. The variations on the basic theme of part-time work appeal to the changing needs of the American work force and have introduced more elasticity into employer practices and job designs, opening up new sources of labor supply within the American labor market.

- Higher fringe-benefit costs per labor hour need not be an obstacle to hiring part-time workers. Practical solutions—prorating, cost-sharing, waivers, and "cafeteria" benefits—have been found for these problems.
- Large-scale use of new schedules appreciably reduces commuting time, saves energy, improves public transport, and lessens air pollution.
- Flexible work schedules are essential to the strengthening of family life, especially now that the structure of families has changed so radically.
- New work schedules allow workers to devote more time to personal needs—social life, leisure, and education—without reducing their commitment to the job.
- Work-sharing, job-sharing, voluntary part-time work and voluntary furloughs hold great promise as methods of softening the impact of business downturns.
- Although it is widely believed that unions oppose the introduction of new work schedules, many unions have been enthusiastic participants provided that they share with management the responsibility for selecting, designing, and implementing them. But unions often oppose plans that are open to the abuse of overtime by employers.

These conclusions have resulted in 50 recommendations by Work in America Institute to labor unions, employers, and government to facilitate the use of new work schedules and to improve their applicability. The recommendations are listed below.

Recommendations

Choosing New Work Schedules

1 Employers and unions deciding on a new work schedule should conduct three sequential investigations:

a. Do we need a new work schedule? The answer depends on whether there are workplace problems that new work schedules can help solve, workplace opportunities that they can help realize, or employee preferences that have been articulated.

    b.   If we need a new work schedule, can any of them succeed here? The answer depends on the technological and social characteristics of the workplace, and on matching both with a particular schedule.

    c.   If one or more new work schedules would succeed here, which one or combination is best for us? The answer is found by assessing the strength of the incentives for, and constraints against, the use of each schedule, as well as the management problems it might entail. *(Page 50)*

2 Employers and unions should give serious consideration to *flexitime* because it is adaptable to a wide range of jobs, employers, and industries, and has been accepted by almost all employees to whom it has been offered. It is less well suited to units where the technology is necessarily continuous process, to machine-paced assembly-line production, or, more generally, to situations where machines rather than people govern the pace of operations. *(Page 52)*

3 Because *flexitime* directly and immediately affects the job of first-line supervisors, employers should institute training programs in advance of a decision to implement flexitime, in order to reorient first-line supervisors to the changed nature of their jobs. *(Page 52)*

4 Those who are charged with responsibility for deciding on a new schedule should ascertain the views of top managers before *flexitime* is adopted and should make sure to clarify for them the relationship between flexibility in working hours and work values. *(Page 53)*

5 Because the more flexible variants of flexitime offer the greatest promise both for economic gains to employers and for improved family life and personal time to workers, we recommend that employers and labor unions work together at local level to reconsider overtime provisions vs. flexibility trade-offs, and at national level to consider whether labor laws can be modified so as to permit more flexible versions of *flexitime* to be used without cost penalty to employers and without loss of benefit to workers. *(Page 53)*

6 We recommend that companies which have continuous-process around-the-clock operations and shift working consider the three-day, 12- (or preferably 12½-) hours-per-day version of *compressed work-weeks* as a suitable solution. This schedule offsets many shortcomings of shift work and provides a better balance between the needs of the plant and the life-styles of workers. *(Page 54)*

7 We recommend that collective agreements and company policies that require overtime pay after eight hours in a day be renegotiated when *compressed weeks* are an attractive option to both union and management. *(Page 55)*

8 Employers and unions should distinguish *permanent part-time* jobs from temporary employment and should define part-time work as a regular employment option having both permanence and career orientation, just as full-time jobs do. *(Page 55)*

9 Employers and unions should regard *part-time employment* as the work schedule of first choice when job tasks are discrete and self-contained, when workers are quite independent of one another, when the demand for output is predictably cyclical, or when the size of the work load is not neatly divisible by a standard allocation of full-time labor. *(Page 56)*

10 Employers and unions should consider *job sharing* as a means of filling jobs that require continuous full-time coverage and extensive on-the-job training. This is a relatively new option with high potential, good productivity results, and rewards for workers and management. *(Page 56)*

11 Employers and unions should join forces to amend federal and state laws so that employers' contributions to statutory fringe benefits are strictly proportional to earnings. *(Page 57)*

12 Labor unions and employers should negotiate *part-time* and *job-sharing* arrangements that meet the desires of existing full-time employees to reduce hours of work, without cutting into opportunities for new full-time and part-time jobs. *(Page 58)*

Managing New Work Patterns

13 Employers, before adopting any new work schedule, should plan for the changes in management practices and philosophies it will entail. *(Page 59)*

14 The employer's first task in implementing *flexitime* should be to ensure the existence of a consensus among top managers that endorses the key flexitime concepts of increased choice and control for workers. *(Page 60)*

15 Before implementing *flexitime*, employers should train supervisors to meet their new responsibilities and problems. *(Page 61)*

16 Employers who adopt *flexitime* should develop an overall strategy embracing the principles and tactical guides described below:

Principles

   a.   Do not overmanage flexitime.

   b.   Decentralize management decisions about the design and operation of flexitime.

   c.   Limit the role of corporate top management to (1) endorsing the flexitime program in principle and in basic outline, (2) providing the resources necessary to plan and carry out the program, and (3) coordinating the design and operation via the human-resources function.

   d.   Invite employee and union participation in the planning, design, and operation of flexitime.

   e.   Explicitly state the reasons why the program is being adopted.

   f.   Organize the human-resource function to achieve the potential gains from flexitime.

   g.   Begin conservatively.

Tactical Guides

   a.   Before implementing flexitime, anticipate and plan for problems of coverage and communication.

   b.   Ask employees to assure that coverage needs are met voluntarily among themselves.

   c.   Clarify who has responsibility and authority for choosing work schedules.

   d.   Let the head of each work unit be the leader and final authority, in cooperation with the union representative, in determining the details of its flexitime program, subject to company-wide guidelines.

   e.   Designate a project leader for the flexitime program to serve as resource person, coordinator, and information source, in cooperation with the union representative.

   f.   Plan supervisory retraining and undertake it before flexitime is implemented.

   g.   Plan cross-training, as needed, and carry it out on the job prior to implementing flexitime.

   h.   Clarify the impact, if any, of labor laws.

   i.   Publish a brief flexitime manual or handbook telling what the program is and how it works.

j. Before all workers go on flexitime, institute a pilot project or experiment for the purpose of solving problems and changing the program's design as required.

k. Design the program, work unit by work unit.

l. Build evaluation of the program into its implementation. *(Pages 61-64)*

17 Employers who wish to employ *part-timers* without incurring excessively higher labor costs per hour should consider three options: (1) prorating of fringe benefits, (2) cost sharing or waiver of fringe benefits, and (3) improved administrative practices. *(Page 65)*

18 Employers should, as a matter of enlightened self-interest, adopt wage, benefit, and other personnel policies which place *part-time employees* on an equal footing with full-timers, despite the superior market power employers enjoy. *(Page 67)*

19 In order to increase the effective integration of *part-time* employees, employers should adopt three policies: paying part-time employees at the same rate as full-time employees for equal skill and responsibility, expansion of the occupational range, and extension of promotional opportunities. *(Page 68)*

20 We recommend that employers and unions give heightened attention to the potential for *job sharing* as a personnel policy which is responsive to changing life-styles and the dual-worker family and is highly adaptable to organizational needs. *(Page 71)*

Seeking Solutions to Energy and Commuting Problems through New Work Schedules

21 State and local governments, in concert with employers and unions, should take the initiative in organizing *area-wide flexitime* programs. It would be particularly helpful if the governments involved were to adopt flexitime for their own employees. *(Page 80)*

22 Local authorities and employers should give preference to *city-wide flexitime* programs over staggered hours as a progressive transportation management strategy. *(Page 81)*

23 As a means of strengthening the impact of an *area-wide flexitime* program:

    a. Mass-transit operators should adopt pricing and marketing strategies that enhance the value of flexitime, for example, by offering, as some cities now do, free or low-cost rides during off-peak hours.

    b. Employers and governments should encourage car and van pooling, for example, by computer matching of sharers, by offering incentives (such as direct payments, use of pooled vans for nonwork life, and preferential or inexpensive parking), by granting social recognition, and by creating priority lanes. *(Page 81)*

24 Local authorities and employers in small and medium-sized cities should adopt *city-wide flexitime* programs, whether or not there are obvious traffic bottlenecks or inadequate public-transportation systems. *(Page 82)*

25 State and local governments, regulatory agencies, and public utilities should join in promoting *area-wide flexitime* and should make it more attractive with price structures that favor use of electricity at nonpeak hours. California's program of low-cost loans by utilities to homeowners, which has helped keep prices down by making additional capacity unnecessary, is a good analogy. *(Page 82)*

26 Since the advantages of *flexiplace* would accrue even more to society than to employers, the federal government and major foundations should sponsor large-scale pilot studies on the technical feasibility of flexiplace, not only in government employment, but also in private employment. Private employers also should introduce such pilot studies. *(Page 84)*

27 We recommend that if at some future time gasoline rationing goes into effect, Congress should enact the *four-day workweek* simultaneously, with each driver's ration based on a 20 percent reduction of commuting travel and no increase in noncommuting travel. *(Page 86)*

28 Every organization should develop and keep up to date a contingency plan under which its employees work a *four-day week*, even if the workplace itself has to remain open five, six, or seven days a week. *(Page 86)*

29 Since commuting adds to the unattractiveness of ten-hour days, employers operating on the *compressed workweek* should, whenever practical, also adopt flexitime or staggered hours, which not only ease commuting but save energy in their own right. *(Page 86)*

30 If it should become necessary to maintain the *four-day week*, Congress should legislate a 36-hour workweek, i.e., a week of four nine-hour days, reducing the traditional 40-hour workweek by one hour a week each year over a period of four years, with no loss in pay. *(Page 86)*

New Work Schedules and Employment Policy

31 The results of the California short-time compensation program for *work sharing*, inconclusive as they are, are good enough to warrant comparable experiments by other states. Active federal encouragement, advice, and (small amounts of) money would speed the process. *(Page 96)*

32 Congress should enact a short-time compensation (STC) law embodying the key provisions of the Schroeder bill: the development of model STC legislation, and grants and technical assistance to states to assist them in developing, enacting, and implementing STC programs. *(Page 97)*

33 Employers should (1) encourage Congress to pass an STC law embodying the key provisions of the Schroeder bill, and (2) experiment with *work sharing* as a practical alternative to layoffs. *(Page 97)*

34 Congress should also consider STC as part of a national anti-recession employment policy and as a possible substitute for some current measures. *(Page 98)*

35 Tax-cost obstacles to *part-time* employment should be removed by computing the employer's contribution on the basis of how many full-time job equivalents are on the payroll, rather than how many actual employees the employer has. *(Page 102)*

36 Congress should remove or significantly reduce the penalty against Social Security annuitants earning in excess of the exempt amount. *(Page 102)*

37 State unemployment laws should be amended to make the availability-for-work requirement for *part-timers* apply to work which is "suitable" in light of individual circumstances. *(Page 102)*

38 Unions should seize the opportunity to gain new members by advocating the cause of the millions of workers who, for reasons of their own, either prefer *permanent part-time* status or choose it as a necessary step toward full-time status. The legitimate interests of part-time workers include an end to wage discrimination, access to better-paying part-time jobs, and more equitable fringe benefits. *(Page 104)*

39 Unions should poll their memberships periodically on issues like part-time employment, reduced workweeks, flexitime, the four-day week, and compensated work sharing as an alternative to layoffs, in order to stay abreast of evolving attitudes and needs. *(Page 104)*

40 *Part-time* workers should be subject to layoff and recall on the same basis as regular full-time employees, that is, according to seniority. *(Page 104)*

Work Schedules and Family Time

41 In dealing with the problem of conflict and tensions between *work life* and *home life*, employers should try to follow a course of action that is facilitating rather than restrictive. Their policies should be designed to increase workers' options and self-management and, at the same time, to enlarge the potential for improved worker performance on the job. *(Page 111)*

42 Employer policies regarding workers' *family life* and *personal time management* problems should be applicable to employees regardless of age, status, or sex, rather than directed only toward women. *(Page 112)*

43 Because so little knowledge has been established regarding the interaction of work and family, employers should take an experimental approach to new work schedules insofar as they are intended to improve the *family life* and *personal time management* problems of workers. *(Page 113)*

44 Employers should try to accommodate the diversity of their employees' *family-time* and *personal-time* needs by offering several new work schedules rather than just one. These may include flexitime, flexiplace, combinations of flexitime with job sharing and career part-time jobs, and compressed workweeks. *(Page 113)*

45 We recommend that employers experiment with various levels of *part-time* work, especially three-quarters time and four-fifths time, to test the attractiveness of various earnings and career prospects. *(Page 114)*

46 We recommend that employers consider compressed workweeks to ease the personal and family dislocations caused by shift work and involuntary overtime. *(Page 114)*

47 In order to understand their employees' work-time/family-time problems, employers should conduct regular surveys on that subject, with the cooperation of the union, where there is one. *(Page 115)*

48 As another means of obtaining information about workers' work and family problems, employers should make use of family-impact studies. *(Page 115)*

Union Concerns: The Dangers of Overtime Abuse

49 Congress should not amend the overtime laws until a formula is found which does not expose workers to exploitation. When a union local wants the *compressed workweek*, or *flexitime* with debits and credits, the laws are not an insuperable bar. True, if the laws were more elastic, employers would find it easier to institute new work schedules unilaterally. However, new work schedules are most effective and durable when adopted by agreement between employer and employees. *(Page 128)*

50 International unions should open discussions with their locals regarding new work schedules and should suggest how individual workers' needs and objections can be met. *(Page 128)*

I.

Time Management in the 1980s

1.
The Work Environment of the 1980s

The world of work in the 1980s differs qualitatively from that of the 1970s, and the differences will grow more pronounced with time. Change is always going on, but the work environment in the decade ahead will have notable new features that need to be understood by employers and public policymakers, as well as by employees and their unions.

Changes are already apparent in the structure of workers' families, workers' expectations regarding work and the workplace, and workers' life-style preferences. These changes are part of a broader current of change in demographics, living standards, the family, and social institutions, but they also reflect the evolution of new values concerning work, leisure, and the family.

Employers, looking at the same current, see other swirls and eddies: increasingly insistent demands for higher productivity and fuller capital utilization; distressing levels of absenteeism and turnover; a labor supply with changing age distribution, skill mix, and personal characteristics.

To make matters worse, energy and transportation problems have put living and commuting patterns under stress for employers and employees alike.

These changes in the work environment place a premium on time management—not in the popular sense of how individuals can use their time more efficiently, but as an organizational phenomenon. Time management implies redesign of organizational authority relationships and the adoption of new employment policies and practices, in order to use the total input of time (worker hours) available to an organization more flexibly and productively.

New work schedules, such as flexible work hours, flexible workplaces, job sharing, four-day workweeks, and innovative shift working, modify the structure of units of work time into forms better adapted to the new environment. Some change the absolute amount of time devoted to work; others change the allocation of that time over periods of a day, week, or year. In addition, many new schedules effect subtle and lasting changes in the relationship of the worker to the workplace. They accommodate changing attitudes, values, and expectations, and demonstrate the responsiveness of the workplace to the society in which it must function.

These are some of the major changes taking place in the lives of workers, which, in turn, affect their behavior at the workplace.

Family Structure

Family structures have become more diverse and unstable. Family members have assumed new economic and domestic roles, setting up new tensions between work life and home life.

The "traditional" family—a husband-breadwinner, a wife-homemaker, and two children—has all but vanished. Only 7 percent of all family units fit this model.

Today's predominant units are husband-wife families with children, in which both parents work outside the home, and husband-wife working families with no children. There are also growing numbers of single people in the country—never married, divorced, separated, or widowed.

The growing diversity of structure among families is matched by their instability. As the rates of divorce and remarriage rise, it becomes ever more likely that an individual will move from one type of family structure to another during his or her lifetime.

Changes in economic participation among families are even more dramatic. The labor-force participation rate of women has been rising for many years, with the largest increases among women with young children. As a consequence, tasks and family behaviors formerly controlled by gender identity have become matters of individual preference. There are dual-earner families and dual-career families in which husband and wife share financial responsibility for the family. Correspondingly, these families are reallocating child-care duties. Among single-parent families, there are growing numbers of single-father families as well as single-mother families, in which *one* parent carries the full load of family and job.

These trends add up to friction between work life and home life. Indeed, 40 percent of all workers in a 1977 national survey reported such conflict, most commonly because of inconvenient or excessive hours of work. The conflicts can only grow worse unless employers adapt to them.

Life-Styles

Surprisingly large numbers of people say they would like to exchange some work time for personal time. Moreover, many actually do so when offered realistic opportunities. Trade-offs between work and personal time are also trade-offs between time and income—less work and less income in exchange for more time. Personal time includes not merely leisure in the sense of amusements and vacations, but also necessary family, household, and child-care tasks, and further education. The willingness of people to make such trade-offs is especially remarkable in view of the uncertain and difficult economic times of the last several years. Women's increased labor-force participation and earnings, and the rise of dual-earner families, probably have much to do with it.

The form in which workers want to take leisure time is also changing. The majority prefer it in larger blocks—more three-day weekends, more personal holidays, and longer vacations, rather than a shortened working day. Although the 40-hour workweek has prevailed since it became the standard, the average number of hours worked per year has declined substantially, mainly as the result of more vacation, more leave days, and more part-time employment. Compressed workweeks and part-time employment, including job sharing, are the new work schedules that best accommodate such preferences.

Personal time is taking on new importance for an ever-increasing number of workers. As lower-level needs for economic security are met, workers turn toward higher-level needs. The remarkable growth in adult education testifies to that.

Expectations

Workers' expectations about work life and the workplace are radically different from those of a decade or a generation ago. They want jobs that provide not only good earnings and fringe benefits, but also dignity, responsibility, and a chance for self-fulfillment. They want more of a say about their jobs and the workplace. In this sense, the work ethic is changing. Belief in the value of hard work continues, but there is no longer unquestioning obedience to the employer's demands.

The mounting demands of organized labor to eliminate mandatory overtime, and the growing resistance to shift work that involves frequent rotations through night and weekend hours, exemplify these changing expectations. So does the spread of flexible working hours, which shifts the decision-making responsibility from supervisors to workers. Former privileges or benefits are increasingly regarded as normal expectations and, in some cases, as entitlements or rights.

Employers are seeking new ways of adapting organizational needs to individual needs. Hard times or not, employees refuse to do all the adapting. Accommodation must be sought. When a popular movie, "9-to-5," portrays flexible work hours, job sharing, and on-site day care as matters of common knowledge, we can be sure that public consciousness has been raised. The film's message, that male bossism is both wrong and unnecessary and that three female clerical employees can improve productivity by adopting new work patterns and meeting other employee wishes, should not be lost. The mushrooming American quality-of-working-life movement is further evidence that mutual adjustment has to be made.

Productivity

Economic pressures on companies are intensifying. While productivity growth has lagged, nominal wage and fringe-benefit costs have been rising. Absenteeism remains at high levels, and turnover becomes ever more costly. These developments combine to drive up unit labor costs, the most important element of total costs for most employers. At the same time the high cost of new capital equipment requires that human resources be more effectively deployed.

The Human-Resource Management Function

The last years of the 1970s witnessed the beginning of what has been termed the renaissance of human-resource management. The concept of workers as resources and as capital in which to invest (and even as assets to be measured and recorded by accountants) is gaining wider acceptance, without detracting from the importance of physical capital, technology, and hard science.

Energy and Transportation

Despite increases in the fuel efficiency of automobiles and shifts toward smaller cars, the cost of commuting by car from home to work will continue to rise. At the same time, public mass transportation in most major cities is in peril; operating costs and capital costs will rise, and fares will rise with them as local governments are increasingly unable or unwilling to cover transit deficits.

Employers have already been responding to workers' commuting problems with mechanisms such as information clearinghouses to encourage car pooling, company-owned vans, and van-pooling programs offered to employees at costs competitive with mass transportation. A new alternative is to reduce the amount of commuting that needs to be done. Here, new work patterns have a role to play. Working at home instead of at the office, or doing a week's work in four days instead of five, are two such examples.

The costs of heating, cooling, lighting, and operating offices and plants are also rising. One possible solution is to reduce the amount of time that facilities are heated, cooled, lighted, and operated, or to use those facilities more intensively and thus lower the utilities cost per unit of product. Another is to redesign facilities in the 1980s to be more energy efficient. New work schedules can clearly contribute to these solutions.

2.
New Work Schedules for the Management of Time

THE STATUS OF NEW WORK PATTERNS

The standard work schedule—the eight-hour day and forty-hour week—has been with us since the depression era of the 1930s, when union strength, backed by legislation, brought it into being. To this day, over 80 percent of all employees, not counting farmers, put in five days a week, and nearly two-thirds of all employees work forty hours in those five days. Work starting time is usually 8:00 a.m., and quitting time is usually 5:00 p.m. Only one worker in eight has any choice about what his or her work schedule will be. Thus, the standard work schedule is marked by uniformity and constancy.

But the environment surrounding the work world is neither uniform nor constant. Massive changes in demography, family structure, economic conditions, life-styles, and workers' expectations have occurred. Pressures, both latent and manifest, are building on employers to respond with changes in the workplace. Absenteeism and turnover have become ever more costly, and resistance to involuntary overtime is spreading. Many employers are recognizing that the quality of work life bears heavily on these problems.

New work schedules are one of the many quality-of-life changes that are now beginning to take hold in the workplace. Several new schedules have emerged, each of which departs from the standard work schedule in a different way. Some change the length of work time. For example, they may require 30 instead of 40 hours a week, or 1,500 instead of 2,000 hours per year (as in part-time employment and job sharing).

Other new schedules change the allocation rather than the length of work time. For example, they call for ten instead of eight hours a day, or four instead of five days a week (as in compressed workweeks).

Some new schedules let the employee assume a degree of control over the allocation of work time (as in flexitime), and some change the location of work, for example, from a central office to either a satellite office or an employee's own home (as in flexiplace). A closer look will reveal what these work schedules are and who is using them.

Part-Time Employment

Part-time employment is an umbrella term that includes all work demanding less than full time. The number of hours varies. In U.S. government statistics, people who work fewer than 35 hours a week have been counted as part-timers. For federal government employees, 32 hours a week is the dividing line between part-time and full-time hours (beginning in 1979). Many companies require that employees work at least 20 hours a week to have part-time status. While neither the idea nor the use of part-time employment overall is new, several ways in which it is now used are new.

The status of the part-time employee is more important than the hours worked. There are two key variables: permanence and choice. Based on these variables, there are several kinds of part-time employment:

Permanent Part-Time Employment. The job and the worker are expected to be part time for a long time; both are regular and stable.

Job Sharing. A new version of permanent part-time employment, in which two (or more) part-timers share one job. The workers are part time while the job is full time.

Work Sharing. A temporary reduction in working hours chosen by a group of employees during economic hard times, usually as an alternative to layoffs.

Temporary Part-Time Employment. The worker is expected to stay at a job only a short time, because the job does not last or the worker does not have a long-term commitment to the labor force (temporary employment can also be full time, of course).

Phased Retirement. Part-time employment chosen by employees who gradually change from full-time to retired status.

Workyear Contracts. Annual agreements between a worker and his or her company about how much time will be put in and where. Usually these agreements, which are rare, involve part-time work distributed in blocks over the year.

Part-time employment is allocated as part day, part week (full day), or part year. Part-timers may or may not have some choice about their working times.

Some uses of permanent part-time employment and job sharing will be discussed in this report, but not all. Case study research on phased retirement is available in Jacobson (1979), information on work sharing in companies in a report by Best (1980), and an introduction to workyear contracts in Teriet (1977).[1]

Flexitime

Flexible work hours (flexitime for short) means that employees choose their starting and quitting times within limits set by management.[2] Flexitime schedules differ in three ways: (1) daily vs. periodic (e.g., weekly or monthly) choice of starting and quitting times; (2) variable vs. constant length of working day (whether credit and debit hours are allowed); and (3) core time—the hours of the day when all employees are required to be present. Here are the different types of flexitime, going from the least to the most flexible:

Flexitour. A form of flexitime that requires employees to choose a starting and quitting time, stick with that schedule for a period, and work eight hours every day.

Gliding Time. Daily variation in starting and quitting times is permitted, but every day still must be eight hours (or another company-set length).

Variable Day. Credit and debit hours are allowed (e.g., an employee can work ten hours one day and six hours another day), as long as the total hours worked are even at the end of the week or month.

Maxiflex. Credit and debit hours are allowed, and core time is not required on all days—for example, core time might not be required on Monday and Friday. Workers can use maxiflex like a compressed workweek.

Flexitime can be used with part-time as well as full-time employment, but flexitime does not change the numbers of hours worked. The variable-day and maxiflex versions enable workers to reallocate their working time over the day or week.

Another new work pattern that looks like flexitime and is sometimes confused with it is *staggered hours.* Staggered hours is a work schedule in which groups of employees regularly arrive at and leave from work at different times established by management. For example, one department's employees may begin work at 8:00 a.m. and leave eight hours later, while another department's employees arrive at 8:30 a.m. and leave eight hours later. The staggered-hours schedule differs from the most conservative flexitime model (flexitour) in that management sets the schedule rather than employees and entire groups of workers follow the same schedule.

Flexiplace. Flexiplace goes a step further than flexitime in that it changes the location of work as well as the working hours. Usually flexiplace means that an employee can work occasionally, or most of the time, or even all the time, at home. Such a work pattern is sometimes called "home work." Another version of flexiplace is the utilization of very small (e.g., one-room) offices at satellite locations close to employees' homes.

Compressed Workweeks

Compressed workweeks refer to full-time work accomplished in less than five days per week. The schedules that are used include (1) four-day workweeks with 10-hour days, (2) three-day workweeks with twelve-hour days, (3) four-and-one-half-day workweeks with four nine-hour days and one four-hour day (usually Friday), (4) the 5/4-9 plan of alternating five-day and four-day workweeks with nine-hour days, and (5) the work weekend of two twelve-hour days, paid at premium rates.

Compressed workweeks do not change the length of work time, nor do they give workers control over their working hours (unless the compressed workweek also explicitly has flexitime); they do reallocate work time over the week. (The "rolling 10/4," a continuous alteration of four ten-hour days on and four days off, falls outside the definition of compressed workweeks, because it shortens the workweek and reduces income correspondingly.)

This detailed listing of categories of new work schedules gives the impression that there are a limited number of discrete types of schedules, among which employers and employees must make limited choices. The appearance is misleading. One of the most exciting developments in the field of new work schedules is the discovery that an almost infinite variety of combinations and permutations is possible. Given enough ingenuity, the parties can develop schedules to meet the most diverse combinations of operating requirements and personal needs.

For example, in West Germany the Mey firm, a small manufacturer of knitwear, allows its operators to have flexitime, part-time work, or flexiplace. Another West German firm, Thomae, is a large pharmaceutical manufacturer. Both its full-time and its part-time operators are on flexitime.[3]

In the United States, a midwestern manufacturer of building materials has compressed workweeks and also a large job-sharing program. At Physio-Control, a small manufacturer of electronic medical instruments, there are three different compressed workweek schedules, plus a few job sharers. Some employees of the County of Santa Clara in California have job-sharing arrangements; others work part time or have voluntary reduced hours. United Airlines in 1980 made use of job sharing as a means of work sharing, to meet the needs of a recession, prevent layoffs, and retain a trained work force.

Take the case of Hewlett-Packard in California. All of its manufacturing employees, as well as its white-collar employees, are on flexitime. People doing blue-collar jobs for which individual flexitime is impractical have a system of group flexitime. Pedigree Pet Foods, in the United Kingdom, operates on the basis of continuous-shift work. Any shift operator, however, is free to swap with any suitable operator on other shifts anywhere in the plant as a means of arranging time off; a system of debits and credits for hours off is followed. In Canada, the Shell chemical plant at Sarnia operates as a continuous-process plant. Each operator works in a pattern which includes both 12-hour shifts and 8-hour days. An elaborate swap system enables operators to be flexible about their days off. In the United Kingdom, another Shell plant (Shell U.K.) on continuous shifts permits each group to choose its own shift system. Currently, seven different shift systems are in use. Each group is responsible for arranging coverage, but each worker has great freedom in arranging time off.

On the basis of these examples, it is clear that the most popular categories of new work schedules—flexitime, compressed workweeks, part time—should be regarded only as a starting point for the design of a system that best suits the needs of a particular plant.

The reason new work schedules are being proposed and used is that employers, unions, and employees are beginning to see that changes will need to be made in the workplace to keep up with changes taking place in society. For employers, new work patterns carry significant economic benefits, although not without some costs (see chapter 4, "Managing New Work Schedules"). For employees, new work schedules offer clear gains; only seldom are there problems or costs. In addition, new work schedules have benefits for society and communities—positive implications for energy, commuting and transportation, earnings, job security, family life, and personal time.

WHO USES NEW WORK SCHEDULES?

In order to answer the question, "Who uses new work schedules?" one must ask several other questions: (1) How many employees are on these alternative work schedules? (2) How many companies use them? (3) What kinds of companies (industry, size) use them? (4) What kinds of employees (occupation, age, sex) have them? What are the growth trends?

Part-Time Employment

In 1977, 22.1 percent of all wage and salary workers, or 17.6 million people, were part-time employees. These figures cover all people who worked less than 35 hours per week, including temporary, intermittent, and involuntary part-time workers. Permanent part-time employees (those who usually and voluntarily work part time) accounted for 13.9 percent, or 11.1 million, of all those who worked. Part-timers averaged about 20 hours per week. The most common time pattern is part day, but many part-time employees also work full days for part of a week (see table 1).

Women outnumbered men as part-time employees by a large margin; people who are young or old are especially likely to be permanent part-time workers (see table 2).

Table 1
Part-Time Employment Models Used, 1977

A.	Type	Total	Men	Women
	All part-time employees			
	Percent of all wage and salary workers	22.1	14.5	32.6
	Number (millions)	17.6	6.7	10.9
	Usual voluntary part-time employees			
	Percent of all who worked	13.9	7.6	22.7
	Number (millions)	11.1	3.5	7.6

B.	Permanent Part-Time Employment Models	Percent of User Firms
	Part day, full week or part week	75
	Full day, part week or part month	49
	Minishift	23
	Job sharing	22

Notes: Data in panel A refer to nonagricultural industries. Part time means 1-34 hours per week. The total in panel B exceeds 100 because the categories are not mutually exclusive and some firms use more than one model.

Sources: William V. Deutermann and Scott Campbell Brown, "Voluntary Part-Time Workers: A Growing Part of the Labor Force," *Monthly Labor Review*, June 1978, pp. 3-10; Stanley D. Nollen and Virginia H. Martin, *Alternative Work Schedules, Part 2: Permanent Part-Time Employment* (New York: AMACOM, a division of American Management Associations, 1978); U.S. Bureau of Labor Statistics.

Table 2
Characteristics of Voluntary Part-Time and Full-Time Workers

Characteristic	Voluntary Part Time (percent)	Full Time (percent)
Marital status and sex—total	100	100
Married men	26	55
Single men	20	11
Women with children ≤ 15 years old	27	12
Other women	27	23
Age and sex—total	100	100
Young men	21	10
Prime-age men	17	39
Older men	8	17
Young women	19	7
Prime-age women	23	19
Older women	13	9

Notes: Data refer to nonagricultural wage and salary workers in 1973. Young age ≤ 25; prime-age=25-49; older age ≥ 50.

Source: John Owen, "Why Part-Time Workers Tend to Be in Low-Wage Jobs," *Monthly Labor Review*, June 1978, pp. 11-14.

Permanent part-time employment was used much more in some industries and occupations than in others. Both wholesale- and retail-trade as well as service industries use large numbers of permanent part-time workers both absolutely and relative to their total employment. Mining and manufacturing are especially low-use industries (see table 3).

A large number of firms (over two-thirds of all companies) have per-

Table 3
Part-Time Employment Usage by Industry and Occupation 1977

| Industry | Usual Voluntary Part-Time | |
	Number (000)	Percent
All nonagricultural industries	10,433	13.3
Mining	17	2.2
Construction	225	5.0
Manufacturing	687	3.4
Transportation, public utilities	334	6.2
Wholesale, retail trade	4,168	25.4
Finance, insurance, real estate	410	9.1
Service industries	4,294	19.9
Public administration	257	5.2
Self-employed	972	16.4
Occupation		
All nonagricultural workers	10,665	13.5
White collar	5,427	13.5
Professional, technical	1,341	10.9
Managerial	328	3.3
Sales	1,166	23.8
Clerical	2,645	17.2
Blue collar	1,981	7.0
Skilled	397	2.9
Operatives, except transport	556	5.5
Transport operatives	300	9.1
Laborers	813	18.9
Service workers, except private household	3,255	31.0

Notes: Data refer to wage and salary workers (except for self-employed line).

Sources: William V. Deutermann and Scott Campbell Brown, "Voluntary Part-Time Workers: A Growing Part of the Labor Force," *Monthly Labor Review,* June 1978, pp. 3-10; and Stanley D. Nollen, Brenda B. Eddy, and Virginia H. Martin,/ *Permanent Part-Time Employment: The Manager's Perspective* (New York: Praeger, 1978).

manent part-time employees, especially in office and clerical jobs; but they have only a few such employees—between 2 and 7 percent in most cases (see table 4).

Permanent part-time employment increased during the 1950s and 1960s, expanding roughly twice as fast as the overall labor force. But there has been no relative growth since then (see figure 1). This pattern holds for both women and men.

Flexitime

In May 1980 the U.S. Bureau of Labor Statistics estimated that 11.9 percent of all full-time nonfarm wage and salary workers were on flexible work schedules.[4] This amounted to 7.6 million people. Of course, many professionals, managers, and sales workers have long had the freedom to set their own hours without calling it flexitime. And indeed, in the government survey, the largest proportion of these workers said they had flexible hours—from 26.5 percent of sales workers to 15.8 percent of professional

Table 4
Number of Firms Using Part-Time Employment,
by Occupation, 1974

Occupation	Percent
All companies	
Production workers	26
Office/clerical workers	64
Professional/technical workers	21
Sales workers	14
Manufacturing firms	
Production workers	30
Office/clerical workers	42
Professional/technical workers	13
Sales workers	9
Nonmanufacturing firms (retailers, banks, service and nonprofit organizations)	
Production workers	20
Office/clerical workers	88
Professional/technical workers	29
Sales workers	21

Source: Bureau of National Affairs, *Bulletin to Management: ASPA-BNA Survey No. 25—Part-Time and Temporary Employees* (Washington, D.C.: Bureau of National Affairs, 1974).

and technical workers. The least usage of flexitime occurred among operatives, only 4.4 percent of whom had flexible hours (see table 5).

There are also differences in flexitime usage rates by industry. By far
the most frequent usage of flexitime occurs in the federal government (excluding the postal service), which is undoubtedly due to the legislatively
authorized experiment with flexitime that began in March 1979. Nearly
25 percent of federal workers reported having flexible schedules. Otherwise
flexitime is most frequently used in finance, insurance, real estate, and other
service industries. The lowest usage of flexitime occurred in the manufacturing industry, where 7.9 percent of manufacturing wage and salary
workers who were full-timers reported flexible schedules.

Figure 1
Growth Of Part-Time Employment

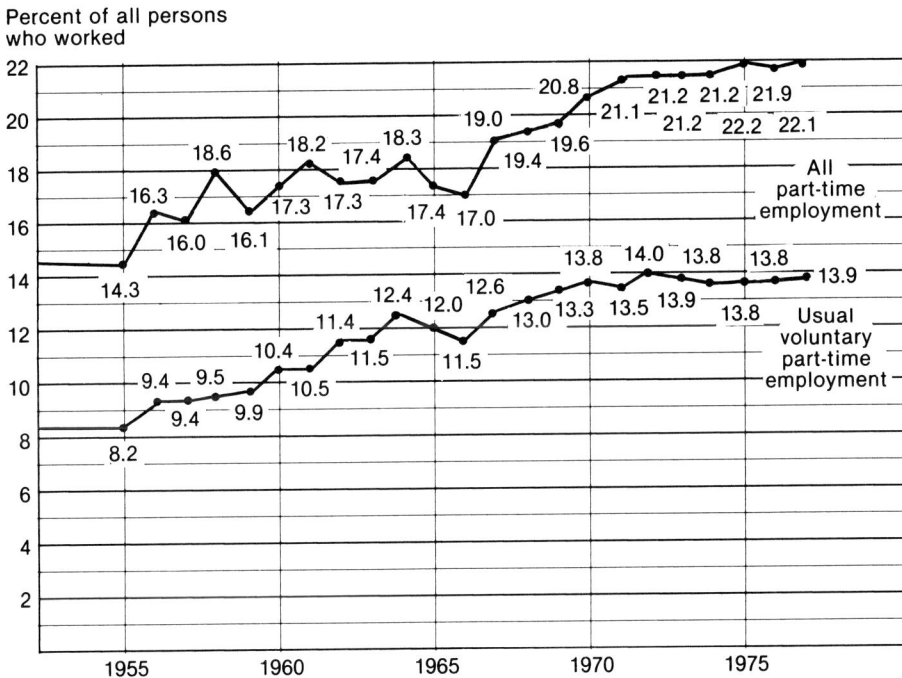

Notes: Beginning in 1966, persons age 14-15 were excluded, thus making data noncom-
parable between the 1954-65 and 1966-77 periods; the trend lines have been roughly adjusted for comparability, although the numbers have not.

Source: William V. Deutermann and Scott Campbell Brown, "Voluntary Part-Time
Workers: A Growing Part of the Labor Force," *Monthly Labor Review,* June 1978, pp. 3-10.

Table 5
Usage of Flexitime in the U.S. by Occupation and Industry, 1980
(Full-Time Nonfarm Wage and Salary Workers)

Occupation and Industry	Number (000)	Percent
All occupations	7,638	11.9
Professional and technical workers	1,914	15.8
Managers and administrators	1,622	20.2
Sales workers	878	26.5
Clerical workers	1,296	9.8
Craft workers	753	7.4
Operatives, except transport equipment	387	4.4
Transport equipment operatives	388	14.3
Laborers	214	7.3
Service workers	569	8.7
Occupations excluding professional and technical workers, managers and administrators, and sales workers	3,608	8.1
All industries	7,922	11.9
Mining	83	10.6
Construction	439	10.1
Manufacturing	1,516	7.9
Transportation and public utilities	620	11.7
Wholesale and retail trade	1,633	4.7
Finance, insurance, and real estate	725	17.1
Professional services	1,555	11.4
Other services	696	16.9
Federal public administration, except postal	404	24.9
Postal service	47	7.6
State public administration	125	14.4
Local public administration	148	8.9

Source: U.S. Bureau of Labor Statistics, news release, February 24, 1981.

The usage of flexitime has increased substantially in recent years. An estimate of flexitime usage by Nollen and Martin (1978) was 5.8 percent of all employees who were not professionals, managers, or sales workers.[5] Thus, if the two surveys can be compared, the increase between 1977 and 1980, from 5.8 percent to 8.1 percent, amounts to a 40 percent rise in frequency of usage (see figure 2).

A smaller proportion of women than men had flexible work hours, and fewer than the average number of young people had flexitime. However, among employees on compressed workweeks, women were more likely to have work-schedule flexibility than men. Labor union members were scarcely more than half as likely to have work-schedule flexibility as non-members. These patterns of usage by sex, age, and union membership reflect the uneven distribution of flexitime among occupations and industries (see table 6).

Among the three major flexitime versions—flexitour, gliding time, and variable day—there was a roughly equal distribution of usage, with perhaps a slight edge for gliding time.

More organizations use flexitime than is suggested by the usage rate among employees. For example, although the usage rate among employees in the 1977 survey was 5.8 percent, the usage rate among organizations in that year was 12.8 percent.[6] This discrepancy is due to the fact that, as a

Figure 2
Growth In Usage of Flexitime
And Compressed Workweeks In The United States

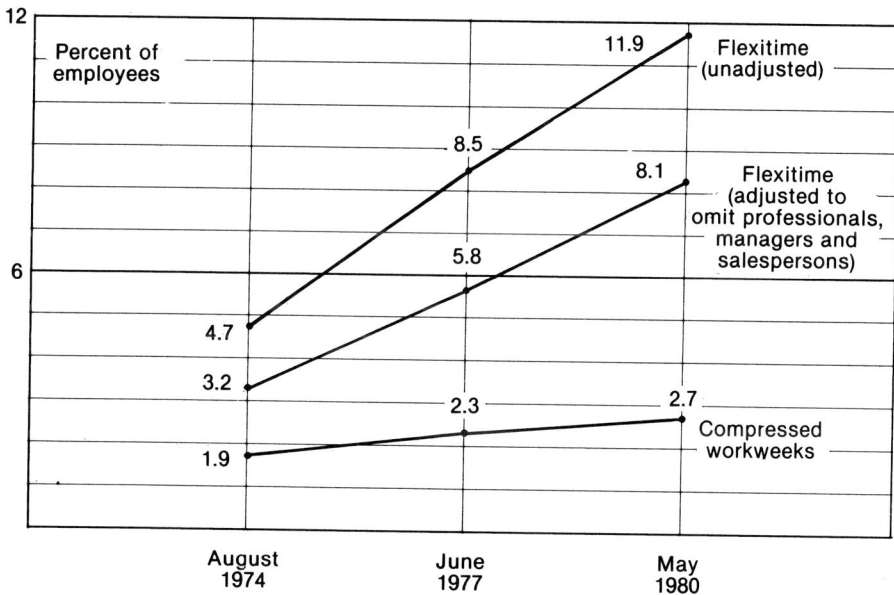

Note: Estimates are obtained from three different surveys whose methodology, coverage, and reliability differ.

Source: For all compressed workweek data: U.S. Bureau of Labor Statistics, news release, February 24, 1981. For flexitime data, for 1980: U.S. Bureau of Labor Statistics, News Release, February 24, 1981; for 1977: Stanley D. Nollen and Virginia H. Martin *Alternative Work Schedules, Part 1: Flexitime.* New York: AMACOM, 1978; Work in America Institute; for 1974: calculated by Stanley D. Nollen from data by Virginia H. Martin; Work in America Institute.

rule, not all employees in a flexitime-user organization are included in the flexitime program. Thus the fraction of organizations in 1980 that used flexitime for at least some of their employees is probably over 20 percent.

As of the middle 1970s, flexitime was very much more widespread in European countries than in the United States, especially in Germany and Switzerland, where one-third or more of the work force was on flexible hours.

Table 6
Usage Rate of Flexitime by Sex, Age, Family Characteristics,
Labor Union Membership, and Days Worked, 1980

Item	Percent on Flexitime
Sex	
Men	13.2
Women	9.8
Age	
16 to 24 years	9.6
25 to 54 years	12.7
55 to 64 years	10.6
65 years and over	14.1
Marital status	
Never married	10.9
Married men, spouse present	13.5
Married women, spouse present	9.5
Other	12.1
Presence of children	
Men with children under 18 years	13.9
Women with children under 18 years	10.1
Without children under 18 years	11.3
Union status	
Union member (includes employee association)	7.3
Other	13.7
Days worked	
4 days per week or less—men	12
4 days per week or less—women	16
5 days per week—men	12
5 days per week—women	9

Note: All data refer to full-time nonfarm wage and salary workers who were at work in the survey week in May 1980.

Source: U.S. Bureau of Labor Statistics, news release, February 24, 1981.

Compressed Workweeks

In 1980, 2.7 percent of all full-time nonfarm wage and salary workers, or more than 1.8 million people, were on compressed workweeks. These figures include work schedules of four and a half days, four days, and three days or less. About two-thirds of all compressed workweek users were on four-day schedules. The 1980 figure, measured in May, represents the first increase in the proportionate usage of compressed workweeks since 1975. Just as the rapid rise in usage of compressed workweeks between 1973 and 1975 was partly due to the new-found concern over gasoline at that time, this sudden upturn may reflect the gasoline shortages of the spring and summer of 1979 (see figure 3).

Figure 3
Growth Of Compressed Workweeks

Percent of all nonfarm wage
and salary workers who
work fulltime

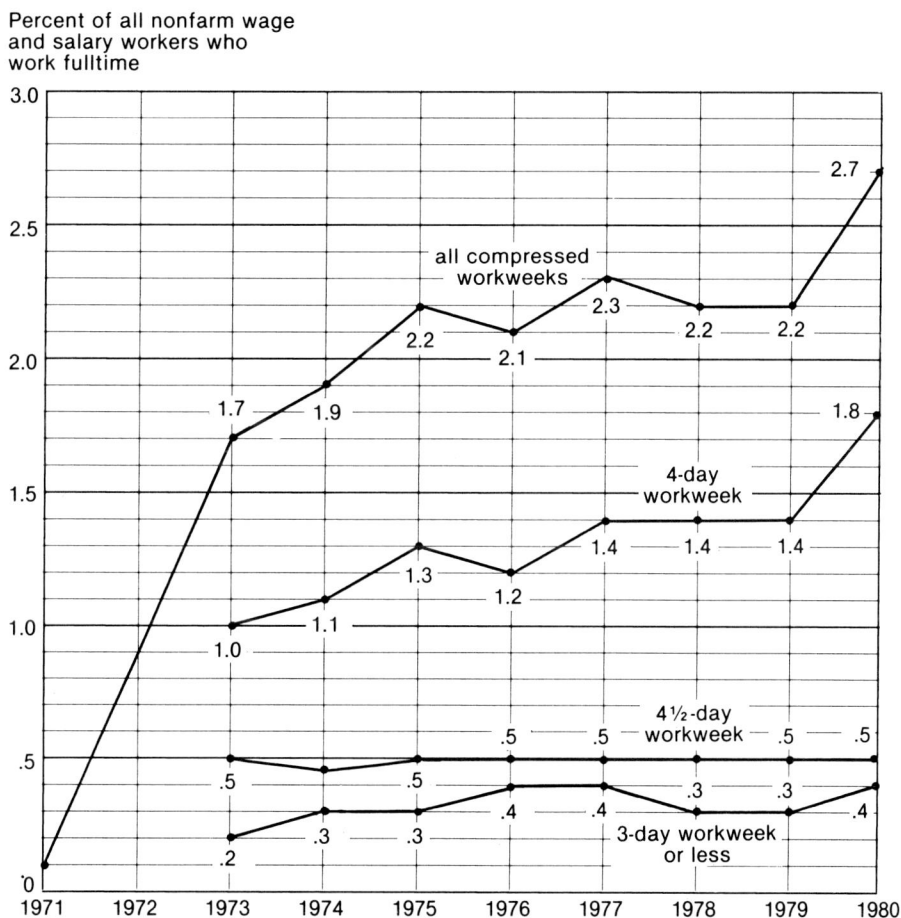

Sources: Janice Neipert Hedges, "How Many Days Make a Workweek?" *Monthly Labor Review*, April 1975, pp. 29-36. U.S. Department of Labor, Bureau of Labor Statistics, news release, February 24, 1981.

Compressed workweeks are used most heavily in local public administration, mainly by police and fire personnel. The smallest use of compressed workweeks occurred in the finance, insurance, and real estate industries. There were also occupational differences in the popularity of compressed workweeks. Service workers (6.7 percent) were most likely to work compressed weeks; administrators and clerical workers the least likely to work compressed weeks (see table 7).

Table 7
Compressed Workweek Usage in the U.S.
by Industry and Occupation, 1980

| Industry | Employees on Workweeks Less Than Five Days | |
	Number (000)	Percent
Mining	17	2.0
Construction	148	3.4
Manufacturing	422	2.2
Transportation, public utilities	143	2.7
Wholesale, retail trade	267	2.4
Finance, insurance, real estate	76	1.8
Professional services	382	2.8
Other services	148	3.6
Federal public administration except postal service	34	2.1
State public administration	31	3.6
Local public administration	180	10.8
Occupation		
Professional and technical	303	2.5
Managers and administrators	88	1.1
Sales workers	63	1.9
Clerical workers	225	1.7
Craftworkers	244	2.4
Operatives	290	3.3
Laborers	73	2.5
Service workers	439	6.7

Note: All figures refer to nonfarm wage and salary workers who usually work full time.

Source: Janice Neipert Hedges, "The Workweek in 1979: Fewer but Longer Workdays," *Monthly Labor Review,* August 1980, pp. 31-33.

Table 8
Usage Rate of Compressed Workweeks
by Characteristics of Employees, 1980

Item	Percent of Compressed Workweeks
Sex	
Men	2.7
Women	2.8
Age	
16 to 24 years	3.0
25 to 54 years	2.7
55 to 64 years	2.0
Marital status	
Never married	2.8
Married, spouse present	2.7
Other	3.0
Union status	
Labor union member (includes employee associations)	2.2
Other	2.9

Note: See notes to table 6, page 34.

Source: U.S. Bureau of Labor Statistics, news release, February 24, 1981.

There were few differences in the frequency of usage of compressed workweeks between men and women of similar marital status. Young workers were more likely to be on compressed schedules than older workers; labor union members were less likely to be on such schedules than non-members (see table 8).

DO NEW WORK SCHEDULES BENEFIT EMPLOYERS?

Hundreds of employers have had experiences with flexible, compressed, and part-time work schedules in the last decade, and many of those experiences have been reported via case study or survey research. We thus have a fairly reliable idea of the advantages and disadvantages that accrue to employers with each of these new schedules. Of course, the advantages or disadvantages cited by any one employer will not be exactly the same as another's.

Advantages and Disadvantages of Flexitime

Flexitime offers employers three great advantages. First, most employers report that flexitime increases morale and job satisfaction for their workers. Thus, as far as the company is concerned, flexitime is a company-provided benefit that workers like, but which costs the company little or nothing. Second, 40 to 50 percent of all employers report increased labor productivity and lower labor costs due to one or more of the following factors: less paid absence and idle time, improved daily organization of work, accommodation of biological clocks, and increased morale and job satisfaction. Third, many employers report a longer-term and less tangible source of gain in the improved management practices that flexitime usually encourages—mainly the shift of supervisory emphasis from negative controlling to positive planning.

Other major gains are noted by a smaller number of employers, and there are some less consequential gains as well. These include easier recruiting (due to lower turnover and to the popularity of flexitime), less overtime pay (due to less absence and higher productivity), better use of production facilities, greater flexibility in scheduling production, and opportunities to extend customer service.

Employers have also had some major problems in connection with flexitime. First, some first-line supervisors are reluctant to embrace flexitime since it may require them to change their methods and work harder at the outset, especially in scheduling production, insuring coverage of functions, and communicating. Another complicating factor—not a consequence of flexitime but a determination that must be made before introducing flexitime—is the necessity of deciding which employees, doing what kinds of jobs, can or cannot use flexitime.

A small minority of the employers using flexitime have found other problems. There may be higher utility and other overhead costs if buildings are kept open longer hours in order to accommodate flexitime workers. Timekeeping costs or effort may be higher if time-accumulating machinery is used, or if some sign-in, sign-out system is tried. Some labor unions dislike versions of flexitime that permit debit and credit hours and thereby change overtime pay practices. And the variable-day and maxiflex versions of flexitime may conflict with labor law that requires overtime pay after eight hours a day for nonexempt workers on government contracts.

Advantages and Disadvantages of Job Sharing
and Permanent Part-Time Employment

In regard to permanent part-time employment and job sharing (exclusive of work sharing and temporary employment), the main advantage to employers is the reduced labor cost, including less overtime, that results from a better match between the size of the work load and the size of the labor force. In other words, part-time employment solves an operational problem.

In addition, part-time employment and job sharing, in some cases, bring about higher productivity by reducing absence and idle time and by promoting greater efficiency in jobs that are either mentally stressful or tedious. Often part-time employees also display higher morale than their full-time counterparts.

For employers, the principal problem that accompanies part-time jobs and job sharing is that of balancing fringe-benefit costs with those paid to full-timers. Since not all fringe benefits can be easily prorated to time actually worked or earnings paid, some sharing arrangement needs to be worked out in order to provide cost parity for employers as well as equity for workers. Another problem is that labor unions often oppose expansion of part-time employment opportunities because they fear it may increase job competition and damage the interests of their full-time members.

Supervisors sometimes experience difficulty because part-time employees are not always present when desired; it may take extra effort to make coverage and communication work smoothly. Job sharing does not present the same problem because the job sharers themselves make these arrangements and the job is staffed on a full-time basis.

Lastly, the training of part-timers is more expensive per worker-hour because it takes longer for training investments to be recovered. Employers often solve this problem by hiring part-timers who are already fully trained.

Advantages and Disadvantages of Compressed Workweeks

For compressed workweeks—whether four-day, three-day, or 5/4-9 schedules—the principal advantage for employers is that production operations can be rationalized, thus raising output and lowering costs. With fewer start-ups and shutdowns, facilities can be utilized more fully. In addition, the morale of compressed-schedule workers is sometimes higher, and paid absences sometimes lower, than under standard work schedules.

The most serious problem occurs when the work schedule does not synchronize with the operating schedule (for example, if a plant runs five days a week and its employees are on a four-day schedule); in this instance, interfacing and coverage problems often appear. Second, labor laws and union contracts may make the use of compressed workweeks uneconomic because the compressed week usually violates rules about paying overtime after eight hours a day or forty hours a week. These rules either have to be set aside through the agreement of management and union or, in the case of collectively bargained agreements, renegotiated. Contractual holiday-pay rules may also cause problems.

Finally, for some kinds of jobs, fatigue at the end of long days may contribute to productivity declines and safety hazards.

DO NEW WORK SCHEDULES BENEFIT EMPLOYEES?

Among the thousands of companies that use one or more new work schedules are millions of employees whose experiences with these schedules have been assessed via survey and case-study research methods. Of course, what is considered a benefit by one employee might be considered a cost by another, depending on personal characteristics. But the outcomes reported here occur often enough and across a wide enough range of personal characteristics to be regarded as likely events.

Advantages and Disadvantages of Flexitime

For flexitime, the chief advantages for workers are, first and foremost, the increase in morale and job satisfaction that almost always occurs. Employees on flexible schedules feel better about their work: they have a renewed sense of self-worth, dignity, and responsibility, largely because flexitime transfers to them some responsibility and control. On a much more concrete level, another principal advantage to employees of flexitime is easier commuting—a reduction in the time it takes to get from home to work and back again, and an easing of the stress and strain of commuting, since trips can be made at the worker's convenience and not at the peak of rush-hour congestion.

A third major gain for employees is that flexitime permits them to spend more time with family members and friends, even though working hours are not reduced in total. A great reduction in stress accompanies this change. In short, flexibility at the workplace enables workers to mesh home-life needs and personal-time needs with workplace needs.

Since an employee in a flexitime company is free to retain his or her previous pattern of fixed arrival and departure times, the only possible disadvantage (and it is rare) lies in synchronizing one employee's schedule with that of others, on or off the job.

Advantages and Disadvantages of Part-Time Employment

The primary advantage of part-time and job-sharing work schedules for employees is that they open up the possibility for certain groups of people to be employed and earn income—something they could not do if the only options were full-time employment or no employment. Among these are parents with young children for whom they are responsible, students, older people, handicapped people, and the working poor. On the opposite side of the coin, part-time jobs and job sharing permit people who are now working full time to achieve a better balance between work life, home life, and personal time, if they wish, by reducing their hours of work.

Part-timers encounter two main problems. First, they find that career paths are hard to follow while remaining a part-time or job-sharing employee. In part, this difficulty is caused by the simple fact of life that someone working only part of the time needs a much longer calendar time to achieve a given level of experience and to earn promotion. To make matters worse, part-timers are stereotyped as different from full-time employees, in that they are not committed to careers and are not permanent. In consequence they receive neither training nor promotion.

While part-time employment helps some people by opening up job opportunities that let them into the labor force, it can also increase job competition for others who are fully employed and need full-time earnings. These full-time workers sometimes find that with the advent of part-time employment the supply of labor increases and standards for pay and benefits are eroded.

Advantages and Disadvantages of Compressed Workweeks

Compressed workweeks appeal to employees principally because they offer leisure time in longer blocks, which is the way most employees prefer it: every weekend (or every other one) is a three-day weekend. The long weekend is treasured especially by younger workers and single workers.

Compressed workweeks are also advantageous in terms of commuting. Four-day workweeks mean traveling from home to work four times instead of five times a week, a 20 percent reduction in distance and time, and a saving in commuting costs, whether in the form of gasoline for a car, or fare for a bus. There are also many cases in which compressed workweeks result in higher morale.

However, there may be disadvantages. Compressed weeks, unlike flexitime, are not always optional. Some workers who are compelled to adopt a compressed schedule may find that family life and personal time have been complicated, especially if they have young children at home or if they normally undertake evening social and civic activities during the week. The longer workday, in most cases, leaves less free time in the early evening for family and personal errands. However, some employers have resolved this problem by either beginning the workday very early in the morning (earlier than 7:00 a.m.) or by having nine-hour days in a 5/4-9 schedule, instead of ten-hour days.

DO NEW WORK SCHEDULES BENEFIT SOCIETY
AND COMMUNITIES?

Many of the benefits that workers derive from new work schedules are also directly translated into gains for society and communities. But aside from these, there are macrosocial gains that stand on their own.

For example, both flexible and compressed work schedules have substantial potential for helping to solve the nation's energy shortage. Flexitime can do this in two ways: encouraging shifts in commuting loads from energy-inefficient, single-driver-car commuting toward car pooling, van pooling, and mass transit; and by smoothing and speeding morning and evening rush-hour transportation, thus making all forms of commuting more efficient. Gains from these sources have been documented in several employer and city-wide experiences.

Less easy to demonstrate, but probably just as real, is the boost in job satisfaction that appears to accompany flexitime almost universally, and the enhanced feeling 'f well-being among employees. These reactions will have their own positi.e effect on the American spirit.

In a similar vein, to the extent that part-time employment and job sharing open up new job opportunities for target groups, society will gain as these people become better able to take care of their own needs. If this increase in labor supply were to bring about increased unemployment, the gain would be offset; but thus far it appears that the effects of part-time employment on the labor market are likely to be favorable as long as there remain a sizable number of people, now working full time, who wish to reduce their hours of work if and when good career part-time job opportunities come along.

Compressed workweeks, like flexitime, have potential for very large energy savings. Twenty percent fewer commuting trips will mean 20 percent or more savings in energy usage (probably due to the spreading of rush-hour congestion for compressed-workweek employees). Conceivably, these employees may increase driving and thus use more gasoline on their day off and on weekends, but here the empirical evidence, which is scant, is mixed. Nevertheless, the potential for large gains remains. In addition, reducing the number of commuting trips will clearly enhance the quality of air in some large and congested cities, and reduce the public and private outlay of funds to achieve this goal.

A further societal gain, which is also an individual gain, may flow from all three of these main work patterns: the increased uptake of education and training opportunities, whether on the job or in formal classroom settings outside. A principal reason why people work part time is that they can devote a major effort toward education while earning money to help pay for it. Employers on flexible work schedules often find that some of their employees, young and old, who may not have done so before, are now taking courses of study in local community colleges on their own. Usually these courses are vocational in content. In other words, certain options—the opportunity to rearrange the distribution of work time over the week, to work less but still earn something, and to work longer on a few days and leave other weekdays completely open for nonwork pursuits—allow large numbers of Americans to grasp the educational opportunities which are so often frustrated by the rigid schedules of educational institutions.

NOTES

1. Beverly Jacobson, *Young Programs for Older Workers.* Van Nostrand Reinhold/Work in America Institute Series (New York: Van Nostrand Reinhold, 1980).

Bernhard Teriet, "Flexiyear Schedules—Only a Matter of Time?" *Monthly Labor Review*, December 1977, pp. 62-65.

Fred Best, *Work Sharing: Policy Options and Assessments* (Kalamazoo, Mich.: Upjohn Institute for Employment Research, 1980).

2. Many short names other than flexitime are in use, such as "flex-hours." The word "Flextime," however, should not be used to describe a work schedule because it is a registered trademark applied to a specific time-accumulating machine.

3. Most of the case studies referred to in this book are reported in greater detail in Stanley Nollen, *New Work Schedules in Practice: Managing Time in a Changing Society*, Van Nostrand Reinhold/Work in America Institute Series (New York: Van Nostrand Reinhold, 1981).

4. U.S. Bureau of Labor Statistics, "Ten Million Americans Work Flexible Schedules, 2 Million Work Full Time in Three to Four-and-a-Half Days." News release, U.S. Department of Labor, Office of Information, Washington, D.C., February 24, 1981.

5. Stanley Nollen and Virginia Hider Martin, *Alternative Work Schedules* (New York: AMACOM, a division of the American Management Associations, 1978).

6. Ibid., p. 12.

II.

Policy Issues
Inside the Organization

3.

Choosing New Work Schedules

Our review of the work environment of the 1980s discloses several fundamental changes: changes in the demography of the labor force and in the structure of families; changes in the life-styles of workers and in their living and commuting patterns; the transformation of workers' expectations into entitlements and rights; the mounting problems of employers with labor performance and work quality; and the new importance of human-resource management. We see new cost pressures on employers, and new roles for workers in the management of the enterprise.

Work schedules are also in the early stages of major change. Several alternatives to the standard fixed-hours schedule of five eight-hour days a week emerged in the 1970s. The most popular of these, flexibility in work times, burst upon the scene early in the decade. Now the novelty of flexitime has worn off and it is developing into a viable method of operation for many companies. Flexiplace has just begun to catch people's imagination. Compressing full-time work schedules into fewer than five days caught on with considerable fanfare in the early and middle 1970s, plateaued for a few years, and is once again on the upswing. The not-so-new schedule of part-time employment has received new attention in the form of permanent part-time employment and a newer concept: job sharing.

Surveys among employers and workers who are following one or more of these alternative work schedules have informed us of their advantages and disadvantages, benefits and costs, opportunities and problems.

But the questions that matter most to managers, labor union leaders, and workers are these: Do we need new work schedules? Can new work

PROs AND CONs OF

PART TIME

PROs:

Employer: Better match between work-load and employee hours. Higher productivity on stressful jobs. Easier recruiting.

Employee: More time for personal interests.

Family: More time for family.

Community: More job opportunities. More flexible hours of business to accommodate the public.

Society: More job opportunities for those who do not want or need full-time jobs.

CONs:

Employer: Fringe-benefit problems. Union opposition. Coverage problems (except with job sharing).

Employee: Stereotyping of low commitment to job. Lower pay and benefits. More difficult career paths.

Family: None.

Community: None.

Society: None.

FLEXITIME

PROs:

Employer: Higher productivity. Higher morale. Better supervisory practices. Less absenteeism and turnover. Easier recruiting. Less overtime.

Employee: Easier commuting. Better work-time/personal-time fit.

Family: Better fit between work and family schedules.

Community: Improved private/public transportation (large scale). More flexible public hours for retail and services.

Society: Improved transportation/energy efficiency.

CONs:

Employer: Need for supervisory reorientation. Conflicts when only part of organization is involved. Higher utility costs (occasionally). Overtime problems (in some programs).

Employee: None (flexitime is at employee's option).

Family: None.

Community: None.

Society: None.

NEW WORK SCHEDULES

COMPRESSED WORKWEEK

PROs:

Employer: Improved plant utilization. More attractive shiftwork.

Employee: Free time in longer blocks. Easier shiftwork. Less commuting.

Family: Family time in longer blocks.

Community: Improved transportation.

Society: Improved transportation/energy efficiency.

CONs:

Employer: Interfacing and coverage problems.

Employee: Fatigue. Inconvenience due to being out of step with others.

Family: Problems when employee has young children at home.

Community: None.

Society: None.

WORK SHARING

PROs:

Employer: Higher morale. Preservation of employee skills. Avoidance of layoff and recall costs. Flexibility in use of people.

Employee: Continued earnings and benefits. Preservation of affirmative action gains. Job security.

Family: Avoidance of family strains due to job loss.

Community: Avoidance of welfare and other service cost increases. Preservation of tax revenues. Less crime.

Society: Protection of affirmative action gains. Less need for public service jobs. Break even on unemployment insurance costs. Less disruption of society.

CONs:

Employer: Cost of fringe benefits.

Employee: Inability in most states to get unemployment insurance benefits. Lower earnings for high-seniority employees.

Family: None.

Community: None.

Society: None.

PROs OF ALL WORK SCHEDULES:

Low capital cost. No need to change organization or technology.

schedules succeed here? If so, which ones are best for us? General statements based on survey findings about how many employers reported what results, and even case-study research about a specific employer's experiences, need to be particularized in order to answer those questions.

This chapter recommends practical strategies that will enable employers, unions, and workers to determine which, if any, new work schedule best suits their needs. It identifies characteristics of workers, workplaces, and the outside environment that are best adapted to each of the major new work schedules.

recommendation 1

Employers and unions deciding on a new work schedule should conduct three sequential investigations:

a.   Do we need a new work schedule? The answer depends on whether there are workplace problems that new work schedules can help solve, workplace opportunities that they can help realize, or employee preferences that have been articulated.

b.   If we need a new work schedule, can any of them succeed here? The answer depends on the technological and social characteristics of the workplace, and on matching both with a particular schedule.

c.   If one or more new work schedules would succeed here, which one or combination is best for us? The answer is found by assessing the strength of the incentives for, and constraints against, the use of each schedule, as well as the management problems it might entail.

DO WE NEED A NEW WORK SCHEDULE?

The proposal to adopt a new work schedule should be in response to an acknowledged problem or need in the company or among the work force rather than a desire to imitate the positive experiences of others. Two kinds of problems involving employee relations or human-resource management are especially amenable to solution by new work schedules. First, there are economic operating problems, such as lagging productivity growth, high rates of lateness, absenteeism, or turnover; difficulty in recruiting quality workers; high labor costs; or excessive overtime payments. Some economic problems stemming from the underutilization of capital equipment (e.g., idle or overused equipment) might also be solved by a different work schedule.

Second, certain behavioral problems, such as low employee morale or declining job satisfaction, an undesirable organizational climate, or ineffective management and supervision, may also furnish an excellent occasion to consider whether new schedules might generally improve employee well-being, management practices, or overall productivity.

CAN NEW WORK SCHEDULES SUCCEED HERE?

Every workplace has both a technical (or economic) component, involving equipment, processes, and costs, and a social (or psychological) component, involving relations among those who do the work and the interrelationships of people and the work technology. Balancing the technical component with the social component is the key to sustained improvement of productivity and quality of working life.

Thus, before choosing a new work pattern the employer and/or union should examine first the technological characteristics of the workplace: interface requirements, output-demand characteristics, work processes, and job interchangeability. They should next examine social and organizational features, such as the demography of the work force, its attitudes and values, the quality of industrial relations, and organizational climate. To these should be added an assessment of the external environment that impinges upon the workplace, including labor law, government policy, labor-market geography and conditions, transportation systems, and energy costs.

WHICH NEW SCHEDULE IS BEST FOR US?

In considering which of several new work schedules could be used, employers and unions should view the choice in terms of three basic options. First, do we want to reallocate work time over the day, week, or year? The schedules that accomplish this are flexitime, flexiplace, staggered hours, and compressed workweeks. Second, do we wish to give workers greater control over their work time? Both flexitime and flexiplace accomplish this. Third, do we want to let employees reduce the number of hours they work? Permanent part-time employment, job sharing and work sharing all do that.

A closer look at the three main new work schedules—flexitime, compressed workweeks, and job sharing—reveals the technical, social, and environmental variables that affect their use.

Flexitime

Flexitime can succeed in blue-collar production jobs as well as in white-collar office jobs. The key technological requirement is a reasonable degree of independence among workers and between jobs. It clearly will not do for workers individually to choose their starting and stopping times if they have to be present when others are present, as in assembly lines. But flexitime is flexible. For example, at the Pedigree Pet Foods plant in Britain, where a vastly expanded and centralized swapping system has been developed in order to permit a degree of flexibility, despite assembly-line production, and at Hewlett-Packard, small groups vary their starting and stopping times jointly. Flexitime can be used easily in assembly operations which are of the batch-process or bench-assembly type and provide sufficient inventories of parts and outputs, as in Sercel Industries.

recommendation 2

Employers and unions should give serious consideration to flexitime because it is adaptable to a wide range of jobs, employers, and industries, and has been accepted by almost all employees to whom it has been offered. It is less well suited to units where the technology is necessarily continuous process, to machine-paced assembly-line production, or, more generally, to situations where machines rather than people govern the pace of operations.

In certain jobs an employee may have to be present during fixed hours to receive visitors or answer telephones; but as long as there is more than one person in the work unit who can do these tasks, a voluntary coverage system can be worked out among the employees themselves to make flexitime possible. Voluntary coverage does limit the degree of choice any one employee has, but it works very well in most cases.

When flexitime comes in, supervisors often fear a loss of control and a weakening of their ability to ensure that the work gets done. In fact, flexitime does require a transfer of some supervisory duties to employees themselves (most notably, part of the control function), but it compensates by making other supervisory functions (such as short-term planning) more important.

recommendation 3

Because flexitime directly and immediately affects the jobs of first-line supervisors, employers should institute training programs in advance of a decision to implement flexitime, in order to reorient first-line supervisors to the changed nature of their jobs.

Managers' views about increasing the decision-making role of workers can make or break flexitime. Even though flexitime represents a rather small and simple alteration in only one aspect of employment policy, it is not uncommon to find senior people regarding it as an erosion of the work ethic and a diminution of management prerogatives.

Those who are charged with responsibility for deciding on a new schedule should ascertain the views of top managers before flexitime is adopted and should make sure to clarify for them the relationship between flexibility in working hours and work values.

recommendation 4

The chief external constraints against the use of flexitime are labor laws that require overtime pay after eight hours in a day or 40 hours in a week, and collective bargaining provisions that do so even if labor law does not apply. Only the variable-day and maxiflex versions of flexitime, which permit debit and credit hours to be carried over for days or weeks, run afoul of overtime law, and that law affects only nonexempt employees (for the 40-hour provision) or nonexempt employees working directly on government contracts (for the eight-hours-a-day provision). However, collective bargaining agreements and in some cases company policy, even in the absence of labor union representation, often extend the reach of overtime pay provisions to include all employees who work more than eight hours a day. Where such overtime provisions remain in effect, flexitime is limited to the gliding time or flexitour versions.

Because the more flexible variants of flexitime offer the greatest promise both for economic gains to employers and for improved family life and personal time to workers, we recommend that employers and labor unions work together at local level to reconsider overtime provisions vs. flexibility trade-offs, and at

recommendation 5

national level to consider whether labor laws can be modified so as to permit more flexible versions of flexitime to be used without cost penalty to employers and without loss of benefit to workers.

Compressed Workweeks

Some work technologies are made to order for compressed workweeks. Where start-ups and shutdowns are costly, when capital equipment is underutilized, or when travel time to job sites is lengthy, compressed workweeks allow work units to rationalize production operations and improve output and efficiency. Employers may be able to cut costs by shutting down on the fifth day of the week, thus saving on utilities and overhead.

The kinds of work units in which compressed workweeks are least likely to succeed are those which have extensive interfaces among different work units in the same company, frequent contact with customers or suppliers, and business functions that need to be covered with full staffing during all usual business hours. In such cases an entire group of workers may be out of step with the rest of the world. In addition, if the work is excessively taxing or tedious, fatigue may set in and productivity may be damaged.

Unlike flexitime, compressed workweeks do not appeal to all employees, although the evidence is not clear-cut (the various surveys and case studies disagree). Some people find that the longer days of compressed workweeks interfere with their personal life and family time. These are likely to be parents with young children. But workers without extensive commitments outside of work find compressed workweeks desirable because it gives them the longer blocks of leisure time which they desire. Some of the objectionable features of compressed weeks may be offset by early starts and finishes, or by applying flexitime rules to the longer working days (as in maxiflex).

recommendation 6

We recommend that companies which have continuous-process around-the-clock operations and shift working consider the three-day, 12- (or preferably 12½-) hours-per-day version of compressed workweeks as a suitable solution. This schedule offsets many shortcomings of shift work and provides a better balance between the needs of the plant and the life-styles of workers.

The experiences of Shell Canada, Physio-Control Corporation, Seattle Water Pollution Control System, Prudential Insurance Company, AT&T and others are convincing evidence that many of the adverse symptoms of shift working can be alleviated or eliminated by changing from the standard five shifts a week, eight hours per shift, rotating schedule to a three-shifts-per-week, 12-hours-per-shift schedule. Still more effective is the schedule of three 12½-hour days. The overlap more than repays its cost by facilitating better communications between shifts, the clearer transmission of instructions, and joint planning.

As shift working expands due to changes in the way production systems operate, and as workers become more hostile toward shift work, this will become an optimum area in which to adopt a compressed work schedule. The compression of the shift-work schedule means fewer working hours outside of the normal workday and fewer times when there is weekend work. With compression, rotations also become less frequent.

To cope with the refusal of many workers to work weekends, several companies in the rubber industry have successfully adopted a special compressed weekend shift of two 12-hour-days, paid at time and one-half. Local unions have accepted the arrangement.

We recommend that collective agreements and company policies that require overtime pay after eight hours in a day be renegotiated when compressed weeks are an attractive option to both union and management.

recommendation 7

Many 12-hour-shift schedules call for more than 40 hours of work in some weeks, which puts them in conflict with the Fair Labor Standards Act. Also the 12-hour-day schedule, four-day workweeks of ten hours each, and the 5/4-9 schedules, which use nine-hour days, may trigger overtime payments. When collective agreements or company policies have been extended to include overtime pay for all hours worked by all people beyond eight in a day, they inhibit compressed weeks. Currently some companies avoid the extra cost of overtime pay by adjusting the base wage rate downward, and then paying premium pay so that the weekly or monthly total earnings for compressed time are no higher than they were for the conventional workweek. This tactic is criticized by some employers and unions. We reiterate the need for employers and unions to join forces in removing the overtime barrier where it works to the detriment of both parties. Premium pay provisions should not be weakened, but neither should they establish an impenetrable barrier to new designs of work schedules attractive to workers and employers.

Permanent Part-Time Employment

Job sharing and other forms of *permanent part-time employment* have been tagged as suitable only for marginal jobs and marginal workers. This is a biased view of part-time employment which is only marginally valid. One reason for the bias is the continuing confusion of part-time employment with temporary employment. While temporary employment, whether full time or part time, is essential in the staffing of almost any enterprise, in this policy study we deal only with *permanent* voluntary part-time employment and job sharing. The second reason is that part-time employment has long been associated with special groups in the labor force, most notably women, students, and retirees. The special work needs of some members of these groups cause part-time to be seen by employers and unions as special-purpose employment.

Employers and unions should distinguish permanent part-time jobs from temporary employment and should define part-time work as a regular employment option having both permanence and career orientation, just as full-time jobs do.

recommendation 8

Some technological conditions make

part-time employment a natural, and even preferable, alternative to full-time employment; other technological conditions make part-time employment difficult to use.

recommendation
9

Employers and unions should regard part-time employment as the work schedule of first choice when job tasks are discrete and self-contained, when workers are quite independent of one another, when the demand for output is predictably cyclical, or when the size of the work load is not neatly divisible by a standard allocation of full-time labor.

The work technologies that favor the use of part-time employment are those that permit the size of the labor input to be more closely tailored to the work load. In some work units this might mean that capital utilization can be improved by using part-time minishifts—a crew of part-timers who work four- or five-hour workdays, before or after the regular day work shift. Part-time employment has been regularized in retail trade, services, government, and financial institutions.

recommendation
10

Employers and unions should consider job sharing as a means of filling jobs that require continuous full-time coverage and extensive on-the-job training. This is a relatively new option with high potential, good productivity results, and rewards for workers and management. Ordinarily such jobs are unsuitable for part-time employment, but job sharing means that the job is staffed on a full-time basis even though job holders are part time.

For example, the Wichita, Kansas, Board of Education accepts teacher-initiated job-sharing arrangements, in which each member receives half the base pay and half the benefits and teaching credits. Fruitful combinations of older and younger teachers have been made possible by a 1978 state law which allows teachers to retire at 60, receive their pensions, and be rehired into any job for which they are qualified.

The feasibility of job sharing depends on whether it is possible to devise good communications systems, to institute a consultative supervisory arrangement, and to have a manageable work schedule. Job sharers require more supervision and/or training at the outset, but often less after they become established.

Job sharers need to be people who can achieve consensus in the practice of their jobs, who can jointly take responsibility for successes and failures, and who can submerge their individual egos to their mutual needs and the job.

Part-time and job sharing employment are most likely to succeed where there are change-oriented managers, employee-centered organizations, and some degree of employee participation in management.

Above all, what determines how successful part-time or job sharing employment can be in a company is whether management regards part-timers as differing from full-timers *only* in the number of hours they work. Part-timers do have other major interests and demands aside from their jobs; that is why they work part time, as a rule. But there is no necessary conflict between their work life and their outside time demands.

Two external constraints work against the use of part-time jobs and job sharing: (1) statutory fringe-benefit costs are higher for some part-time employees than for full-time, and (2) some labor unions oppose expanding the use of part-time employment. These fringe benefits, over which companies have no control—Social Security, unemployment insurance, and workers' compensation—are paid for by a tax on earnings up to a ceiling, above which no tax is paid. The result is higher fringe-benefit costs per labor-hour to the employer for workers whose annual earnings are below the ceiling. In a job whose annual salary exceeds the ceilings, two part-time employees can cost more for statutory benefits than one full-time employee.

Employers and unions should join forces to amend federal and state laws so that employers' contributions to statutory fringe benefits are strictly proportional to earnings.

recommendation 11

Proportional taxation as a constant percent of earnings with no ceiling would equalize statutory benefits costs for part-time and full-time employees. The tax rate would fall as higher earnings were taxed, leaving total tax revenues unchanged. The fact that the Social Security income ceiling is scheduled to rise faster than anticipated earnings levels will reduce the frequency of higher costs to employers, but even the higher ceiling will discourage employers from staffing the best jobs on a part-time or job sharing basis. For unemployment insurance and workers' compensation, the tax could be based on aggregate payroll instead of on individual workers' earnings.

Labor unions have opposed the expansion of part-time job opportunities because they believe it will increase the competition for jobs and damage the employment prospects of people who need full-time earnings. Several employers, with labor union initiative and cooperation, have shown how these effects can be minimized. For example, the County of Santa Clara (California) and the Service Employees International Union have collective bargaining agreements under which permanent part-time and job-sharing arrangements are available to employees *only* after they have been with the union and the company for a specified period of time. Thus new employment for full-timers is not weakened, but they are free to reduce their hours and make room for a larger number of employees.

recommendation
12

Labor unions and employers should negotiate part-time and job-sharing arrangements that meet the desires of existing full-time employees to reduce hours of work, without cutting into opportunities for new full-time and part-time jobs.

A promising new application of job sharing as an alternative to layoff is in combination with work sharing (which is itself an alternative to layoffs). The case of United Airlines and the Association of Flight Attendants has demonstrated that in times of economic downturn and threatened layoff a substantial number of people would volunteer to reduce their work time temporarily so that other employees who were to be dismissed or laid off could share the work. Job sharing is attractive because it preserves individual choice (albeit choice constrained by grim alternatives) in the face of economic adversity and permits group cooperation across broad occupational categories. The employer preserves a trained work force and adjusts personnel costs to the recession without painful and costly layoffs. The union retains membership. The workers share jobs, accept temporary leisure/income trade-offs, and ride out the recession without breaking the continuity of career employment.

4.
Managing New Work Schedules

Having selected a new work schedule, the employer will be concerned with launching it successfully and then managing it over the long term, in order to ensure that the maximum benefits the new schedule offers are achieved and that its potential costs and problems are minimized or avoided.

Changes in management practice will probably be needed for any new schedule. Most of these changes will be in the direction of more self-management by employees and supervisors and less control from the center or top of the company. Other changes may be needed in management philosophy, style, values, attitudes, and organizational climate. The new schedules put a premium on more trust and responsibility, more communication in all directions, more adaptability toward workers' needs, and more equity.

Employers, before adopting any new work schedule, should plan for the changes in management practices and philosophies it will entail. Each schedule, naturally, presents its own specific management problems and opportunities.

recommendation
13

MANAGING FLEXITIME

Two essential points in managing flexible work schedules are (1) ensuring that higher managers are in tune with the principle of increased self-management by employees, and (2) assisting first-line supervisors to reorient themselves to their changed jobs.

The most carefully worked out economic plan to introduce flexitime will come to nothing unless top management endorses the idea of flexibility in workers' schedules. The most rigorously documented needs assessment that calls for the implementation of flexitime will be rejected if top managers oppose transferring increased control and decision making to workers.

recommendation
14

The employer's first task in implementing flexitime should be to ensure the existence of a consensus among top managers that endorses the key flexitime concepts of increased choice and control for workers.

It is a fact that flexitime transfers a measure of control over work life from managers to workers. It is also a fact that under flexitime discipline and firm adherence to the work ethic may, to some skeptics, appear to be eroding. Some top managers tend to equate flexibility with laxity, and self-management with chaos. Neither of these equations is necessarily true. Productivity can be increased by letting workers sort out their own work schedules, and labor costs can be decreased by reducing the amount of supervision. The first task for the managers of flexitime is to clarify the relationships between flexitime and the work ethic, management rights, and authority. Doing this requires knowledge of top-management values about work and people.

Success with flexitime requires an organizational climate characterized by a high degree of trust and responsibility in workers, with few rules and mechanistic procedures. It must also manifest a belief in social equality without regard to managerial rank.

The ability of employees to manage themselves will be enhanced if they are trained to plan, set, and measure their own work. Key measurements of white-collar output include: accuracy, timeliness, completeness, and cost effectiveness.

First-line supervision is the critical link in the success of flexitime. Under flexitime the supervisor's role as an intermediary between company and worker becomes more difficult, demanding new functions and new skills. The supervisor loses authority over workers' schedules but continues to be charged with delivering good business results. At the same time, he or she must ensure that workers have genuine flexibility and free choice.

With more decision-making power in employees' hands, the supervisor must exercise control in a more positive way. The supervisor must spend more time and do better at planning and coordinating. The organizing function also changes; there are fewer day-to-day scheduling decisions to make, but more medium- to long-term responsibilities. Directing and leading assume new importance, partly because formal rules are relaxed and workers require a clearer understanding of what is required of them.

These changes amount to an upward shift in the status of supervisors' jobs, despite the immediate impression that they are losing power. Their skills need to be strengthened by training to enable them to understand the nature of power, to cope with uncertainty, and to help them to do a better job of communicating, leading, planning, and evaluating.

Before implementing flexitime, employers should train supervisors to meet their new responsibilities and problems.

recommendation 15

Aside from the overriding importance of management values and supervisory reorientation, successful implementation of flexitime requires a strategic management plan, first, and a set of tactical guides.

Employers who adopt flexitime should develop an overall strategy embracing the principles and tactical guides described below:
Principles

recommendation 16

a. *Do not overmanage flexitime.* It is a simple innovation whose success depends on trust and cooperation. Overengineering this system with detailed rules and regulations is both unnecessary and counterproductive. Employees usually manage themselves and their work better than expected, provided that they understand what is required.

b. *Decentralize management decisions about the design and operation of flexitime.* Let individual work units make most decisions, within basic corporate guidelines. The work schedules of any unit must fit its business needs.

c. *Limit the role of corporate top management to (1) endorsing the flexitime program in principle and in basic outline, (2) providing the resources necessary to plan and carry out the program, and (3) coordinating the design and operation via the human-resources function.* The individual variations in flexitime, necessary for different work units, argue against top management control.

d. *Invite employee and union participation in the planning, design, and operation of flexitime.* Participation is helpful because the program affects employees directly, must be responsive to their needs, requires a measure of self-management to succeed, and is in the spirit of greater employee choice and responsibility.

e. *Explicitly state the reasons why the program is being adopted.* This is for the benefit of management as well as workers. The objectives should be cast in terms of recognized company or workers' problems that flexitime is expected to solve, and/or opportunities to be realized.

f. *Organize the human-resource function to achieve the potential gains from flexitime.* Focus first on business problems to be solved, but do not lose sight of positive spillover effects. Adopt a systems approach, linking flexitime to other human-resource programs. Use flexitime as the opening wedge for further initiatives in organizational development.

g. Begin conservatively. Once flexitime is introduced, it will be difficult to pull back or restrict it. But make sure that the initial flexitime program departs substantially from the old fixed-work schedule and that management practices reflect flexibility. The more liberal the program, the greater the potential for improving productivity and employee well-being, so progressive changes and liberalizations of the initial program should be anticipated.

Tactical Guides

a. Before implementing flexitime, anticipate and plan for problems of coverage and communication. Ask each work unit to determine its coverage and communication needs, and set the limits of flexibility for each affected job category. Set the limits generously: old work schedules often demand coverage beyond what is really necessary.

b. Ask employees to assure that coverage needs are met voluntarily among themselves. This self-selected form of flexibility is better than excluding particular employees from the flexitime program.

c. Clarify who has responsibility and authority for choosing work schedules. To what extent can supervisors set workers' schedules, as against workers setting their own? The guiding principle should be that supervisors determine the actual business needs that employees' schedules must meet, but, beyond that, working hours are up to the employees.

d. Let the head of each work unit be the leader and final authority, in cooperation with the union representative, in determining the details of its flexitime program subject to company-wide guidelines. But insist that employees be genuinely consulted in the design of the program and in problem solving afterwards. Form an employee council or planning committee to ensure that workers' preferences are presented. If workers are represented by a labor union, include union officials in early planning.

e. Designate a project leader for the flexitime program to serve as resource person, coordinator, and information source, in cooperation with the union representative. This person may also mediate conflicts and ensure that company-wide guidelines are observed. Final decisions are usually better left with work units, departments, or divisions.

f. Plan supervisory retraining and undertake it before flexitime is implemented. Most supervisors will benefit from this training. The objectives should be (1) to show supervisors how to ensure their employees' new freedom of choice while still guaranteeing that production/services operate smoothly in the absence of fixed work schedules, (2) to relieve fears of potential loss of control and authority, and (3) to inform them how their jobs will change and instruct them how to accomplish their new tasks. The training can be in-house and short-term (between one-half and three days) but should be formal.

g. Plan cross-training, as needed, and carry it out on the job prior to implementing flexitime. Cross-training is mainly the familiarizing of one employee with the job of another, so that coverage can be maintained.

h. Clarify the impact, if any, of labor laws. If variable-day flexitime is adopted, ascertain whether any affected employees are working directly on government contracts and might therefore have to be paid overtime. If weekly hours are variable, the Fair Labor Standards Act requires overtime for hours in excess of 40 for nonexempt employees.

i. Publish a brief flexitime manual or handbook telling what the program is and how it works. The manual should set out the company-wide guidelines, the role of the project leader, rules governing coverage, limits of flexibility, details of flexible schedules, and employee rights and responsibilities.

j. Before all workers go on flexitime, institute a pilot project or experiment for the purpose of solving problems and changing the program's design as required. Do not adopt flexitime tentatively, nor threaten employees with dropping flexitime if problems occur. Rather, indicate that the design of the program will change as needed, based on early experiences.

k. Design the program, work unit by work unit. The following factors may vary across work units and therefore need to be explicitly dealt with:

- Core hours—hours when everyone must be present.
- Band width—how wide the flexible periods are.
- Lunch period—flexible, or set by employer.
- Daily flexibility vs. weekly or monthly choice of schedule.
- Day length—debit and credit hours permitted, or not.
- Advance notice by employee to supervisor required, or not.
- Timekeeping methods, if any.
- Disciplinary procedures.

l. Build evaluation of the program into its implementation. Some evaluation guidelines are:

- Evaluate the program against its objectives, which may vary across work units.
- Use a combination of subjective opinion or attitude data and quantitative measures of outcomes.
- Collect base-line data to permit before-after comparisons; compare flexitime with nonflexitime groups to pinpoint the effects due to flexitime.
- Use evaluation results to improve the program's design; feed the results back to employees and unions.

- Relate the effects of flexitime to the characteristics of workers and the technology of the work setting.
- Measure indirect and spillover effects, good and bad, as well as intended direct effects. Adopt a comprehensive cost/benefit framework, netting losses against gains to get a single bottom-line outcome.
- Wait long enough for effects to become manifest.

MANAGING PART-TIME EMPLOYMENT AND JOB SHARING

The main management problems associated with part-time and job-sharing employment are: the potentially higher fixed labor costs of part-time employment; the stereotypes of part-time and job-sharing employees as being somehow inferior to full-time employees; and some day-to-day supervisory problems that are peculiar to job sharing, such as brokering, complementarity, scheduling, and communication.

The principal economic issue affecting the use of part-time employment and job sharing is their potentially higher labor cost, owing to the fact that some labor costs are fixed per employee, regardless of the number of hours worked per week. Since part-time employees work fewer hours than full-timers, their hourly cost can be higher. These higher hourly costs are due mainly to the disproportionate costs of fringe benefits and personnel administration.

Fringe benefits paid on the basis of salary or time worked can be easily prorated for part-time work and thus raise no special problems for employers, although some unions frown on this practice. These include vacations, holidays, sick leave, group life insurance, retirement plan, stock options, and profit sharing. Prorating equalizes fringe benefit cost per labor hour for part-time and full-time workers.

Many employers already prorate benefits—ranging from a high of 75 percent offering prorated vacations down to a low of 27 percent offering prorated life insurance (24 percent provide full life insurance coverage, while 49 percent make no life insurance available).[1]

Other fringe benefits do not lend themselves to prorating. Statutory benefits (those required by law) are, as noted earlier, a case in point. Current contribution formulas for Social Security, unemployment insurance, and workers' compensation are regressive, with earning ceilings above which no tax is paid. The employer pays higher fringe-benefit costs per labor-hour for workers whose annual earnings are below the ceiling. In jobs with annual full-time equivalent earnings above the ceiling, two part-time employees incur higher statutory benefits costs than one full-time employee.

By far the most troublesome fringe-benefit cost for part-time employment is group health insurance, which is the most costly for employers and is rapidly becoming more so. While no law requires employers to provide it, as a matter of fact almost all do—to full-timers; but only half the employers offer it to part-timers. Employers who provide it incur an extra cost of $600 to $1,200 per year for each part-time employee who receives the benefit on the same terms as full-timers: the premium is fixed per employee, without regard to earnings or hours worked.

Other personnel administration costs that are fixed per employee and may raise the cost of employing part-timers, are recruiting, training, and record keeping. In addition, costs of supervision and of equipment and facilities may be higher. In some cases, where part-timers are in excess supply and have superior qualifications, employers experienced in using them have reported lower recruiting and training costs than for full-time employees. Generally, however, these costs tend to be higher simply because part-time employment (and especially job sharing) increases the number of employees, which means more recruiting, training, record keeping, supervision, and facilities.

Employers who wish to employ part-timers without incurring excessively higher labor costs per hour should consider three options: (1) prorating of fringe benefits, (2) cost sharing or waiver of fringe benefits, and (3) improved administrative practices. These options are described more fully below.

recommendation 17

1. *Offer the regular fringe benefits to part-time employees where possible, on a prorated basis.* For example, inclusion of part-time employees who work 1,000 or more hours a year in qualified retirement plans has already been mandated by the Employee Retirement Income Security Act of 1974.

2. *If fringe benefits cannot be prorated, offer them on a cost-sharing or waiver basis.* Group health insurance, as noted above, has a fixed premium per employee. The cost-sharing/waiver approach requires part-time employees to choose between paying a higher proportion of the insurance premium than full-time employees, so that the employer's contribution per labor-hour is not raised, or waiving that benefit in favor of a different added benefit. For example, if the employer and full-time workers each pay one-half the health insurance premium, then half-time workers might pay three-fourths the premium while the employer pays one-fourth. If the employer pays the entire premium for full-time workers, then half-time workers might instead pay one-half the premium. If part-time workers choose not to pay the higher premium, they may have the option to apply the value of the forgone benefit to a different one, such as additional days of vacation.

Another approach to equalizing fringe-benefit costs per labor-hour for all workers is a "cafeteria plan" with employer-imposed minimum protections. This is a long-term approach which has the potential to reduce total fringe-benefit costs while increasing employee options.

A cafeteria plan establishes the total dollar value of company contributions to all current as well as prospective fringe benefits, sometimes with a deduction for the additional administrative costs. To ensure that employee income security and business productivity needs are met, minimum levels of participation in some benefits might be mandated by employer policy, such as inclusion in a retirement plan and vacation days. Part-time employees might receive a benefit allowance proportional to their employment and make choices within this allowance.

Cafeteria plans permit new benefits to be offered that are important to some, but not all, workers—for example, subsidized child care or athletic clubs—and they need not cost more. The extra costs of statutory fringe benefits under existing law might also be equalized in this way.

A few employers have used cafeteria benefit plans successfully for many years, since the advent of the computer. Interest appears to be growing. However, some have reported that employees, especially younger ones, often prejudice their future security by making poor choices. The long-term actuarial impacts on small companies also need careful assessment.

3. *Reduce personnel administration costs that are fixed per employee through changes in business practices.*

Recruiting. When recruiting costs for part-time workers are high, it is either because conventional methods for locating job applicants are unsuccessful or because more people have to be recruited. Employers can reduce the costs by using specialized part-time and job-sharing placement services, posting part-time opportunities for present employees, and ensuring that wage and benefit packages are high enough to retain part-timers. They should urge public and private agencies to integrate part-time with full-time placement services. In the long run, the best way to reduce recruiting costs is to make part-time employment a regular employment option that people know about. This will both increase the labor supply to the firm and make it easier for the employer to tap it.

Training. It takes longer for the company to recover its investment in training part-timers because training costs as much for them as for full-timers, but part-timers work fewer hours per year. Training costs for part-time employees can be reduced by pooling their training with that for other employees, and by providing some in-house training on the part-time workers' own time. People who are already fully qualified and experienced, or who learn very quickly, often select themselves for part-time employment and thus may need less training than full-timers.

Record keeping. The cost of record keeping for part-timers is a problem only if manual or inefficient systems are used. Costs for part-time employees can be reduced by automating their records and including them in the same system that handles full-time employees' records.

Supervision. The fact that part-time workers are not always present and that there are more of them compared to full-time staff, can make supervision more costly; but it need not, if part-timers supervise themselves. Increasing the degree of self-management for part-time (and full-time) employees reduces the amount of supervision they require.

Equipment and facilities. When part-time employment raises problems of equipment and facilities, the solution lies in scheduling part-time work with those needs in mind. An employer can use minishifts after regular hours or on weekends; use job sharing with shared facilities and coordinated use; or use flexiplace to avoid adding office or plant space. On the other hand, employment of part-timers often enables an employer to utilize plant more fully than would be possible with full-timers only.

A discussion of the higher labor costs of part-time employment may strike some employers as irrelevant. More often than not, part-timers receive lower pay and benefits than full-timers, one major reason being the higher fixed costs of employing them. If part-timers cost more to use, they get less monetary compensation to even out the equation, unless they have special skills or demonstrate superior productivity.

Another market-based reason why part-timers often do not match full-timers in monetary rewards is that their labor is normally in excess supply, a condition which depresses wages without regard to equal qualifications. And, according to the old "compensating differences" argument, part-time workers often accept lower pay because working only part time enables them to do other things in their nonwork life and thus earn "psychic income."

Employers should rethink their market assessment of part-time work, however, in the light of the changing conditions of the 1980s. In California, often a forerunner of social change, the competitive market for permanent part-timers is much stronger than in the rest of the United States.

Regrettably, the rational grounds for inferior economic rewards to part-timers have three irrational and harmful outcomes: (1) part-time employees are occupationally segregated into low-paying jobs, often unjustifiably; (2) they lack advancement opportunities, or fail to take those that are available; and (3) they suffer discrimination in wages and fringe benefits even after cost differences have been taken into account.

Employers should, as a matter of enlightened self-interest, adopt wage, benefit, and other personnel policies which place part-time employees on an equal footing with full-timers, despite the superior market power employers enjoy.

recommendation
18

Fair and equal treatment of part-time employees makes sense as human-resource management. Giving them access to a wide range of job and training opportunities within the constraints of the marketplace increases the number and range of skilled people available to the employer. Equal treatment and compensation will surely increase their stability, performance, loyalty, and dedication to the enterprise.

recommendation
19

In order to increase the effective integration of part-time employees, employers should adopt three policies: paying part-time employees at the same rate as full-time employees for equal skill and responsibility, expansion of the occupational range, and extension of promotional opportunities.

1. *Pay Policy.* Analyze jobs to ensure that equal tasks and skills are equally compensated, as between part-time and full-time employees. Even if legislation requiring equal pay for equal work covered part-time employees, which it does not, part-timers would probably gain little because the work assigned them is often unequal. Stereotypes about part-time work as "low level" or "unimportant" can be broken down if companies (a) analyze jobs in terms of tasks and functions, (b) analyze the skills needed to perform the tasks and functions, and (c) pay job holders on the basis of how much they know about their job and what they produce.

2. *Occupational Range.* Broaden the range of jobs open to part-time staff to include some management jobs and a greater number and variety of professional and craft jobs.

The existing concentration of part-time workers in clerical, sales, and manual-labor jobs is partly due to the nature of the part-time labor force (many of whom are women and students), partly due to real job requirements (some tasks are done better on a full-time basis), and partly due to employers' stereotypes about part-time employment. Job analysis is one way to make objective decisions about the fit between job requirements and part-time staffing. Job sharing helps to overcome some of the genuine problems that arise when jobs that need full-time attention are given to two part-time employees.

Many employers already employ part-timers in a wide range of professional, technical and managerial jobs, sometimes as individuals and sometimes as job sharers. For example, most of the growth in the federal government's employment of part-timers has been at higher grade levels. Eleven state governments have opened up high-level professional positions. *Control Data Corporation* employs part-timers as accountants, programmers, and personnel administrators. Elsewhere in the private and public sectors administrators, analysts, planners, social service workers, lawyers, engineers, librarians, teachers, and physicians and other health-care professionals are sometimes employed on a part-time basis.

In addition, part-time employees have been able to succeed as supervisors of other professional or highly trained staff, whether full time or part time. However, this use of part-timers requires a more than usual amount of planning, organization and communication in order to work well.

Job sharing is more likely to be a workable solution for management positions. Our casebook, for example, describes three job-sharing teams who supervise other employees, usually full-timers. One team functions as office managers at Stanford University Graduate School of Business. Another team acts as deputy director of legislation in the California Department of Employment Development. The third team directs the Office of Personnel Development in a large eastern university. Two of the teams are responsible for budgets of half a million dollars.

The casebook for this study, *New Work Schedules in Practice*, also describes job-sharing teams that fill high-level professional positions.[2] One team acts as organizational-development consultant for the City of Palo Alto, California, and is responsible for maintaining liaison between the city manager and the city department heads. Other teams function jointly as full-time physicians, social case workers, and teachers, an occupation in which job sharing has been widely accepted.

3. *Promotional Opportunity*. Make promotion and advancement opportunities available to all job holders without regard to current part-time or full-time status.

In order for part-time employees to receive equal work over the long run, they must have access to the training and work experience that is prerequisite to advancement. Employers overlook promising talent if they assume that part-time employees are uninterested in career development.

Part-timers must be encouraged to seek these opportunities and adopt a long-run career posture toward their work if they expect promotion. Bear in mind two important facts: (1) investments by the employer in career development for part-time employees are likely to be more expensive per labor-hour, and this may require cost sharing by employees, or bigger payoffs to the employer from training; and (2) it will ordinarily take more calendar time for part-time employees to achieve the same proficiency as full-time employees, and so advancement may come more slowly.

Job Sharing—Some Special Problems

Job sharing presents a number of management problems: (1) brokering—getting the right match between the workers as partners and between the workers and the job; (2) complementarity—ensuring that workers perform cooperatively (each job sharer has to accept responsibility for the whole job as well as his or her own part); (3) scheduling—deciding who will work when; (4) communication—making sure that each job sharer knows what the other is doing and that both give clear messages to co-workers and managers.

The elements of brokering include: task analysis of the job, assessment of the skills required, and careful recruitment and interviewing procedures.

In the past, most cases of job sharing have been initiated by workers. Increasingly, however, employers have been taking the lead, and a necessary first step is careful task analysis of the positions being considered. This has the virtue of defining duties, clarifying job descriptions and forming the basis for measuring performance.

After analyzing the job, the organization and the job-sharing applicants together verify the skills that workers must provide and judge what contribution each sharer must make. For many jobs—as for example, computer programmers, clerks, social workers, bank tellers—the two members of a team should have almost identical skills. For other jobs, the employer may want a team whose members have different but complementary skills, so that the job is covered with a broader range of expertise. For example, the team hired to coordinate the renovation of a research laboratory and medical school consisted of a mechanical engineer and a Ph.D. who specialized in anatomy. In another case, a publisher with an assistant editor's job to fill hired a team consisting of a former school teacher and a former librarian.

As a rule, the recruiting of a job-sharing team is carried out by a current employee who wishes to reduce hours. Some employers advertise jobs as open to both part-timers and full-timers, which enables them to fill the job in either way.

In the course of recruiting, the employer and the team must reach agreement on (1) schedules, including coverage for illness, emergency, and personal needs; (2) the division of task responsibility; (3) how to ensure communication with supervisors and co-workers; and (4) accountability for raises, promotions, and firing.

How cooperatively the team performs depends on organizational factors as well as the personal relations between job sharers. Support from the immediate supervisor of the team is crucial. It is most likely to be forthcoming when the supervisor is informed about job sharing and the variety of ways in which it can be implemented, and has a part in designing the job and selecting the sharers. It also helps if the supervisor is personally familiar with one or both members of the team. Surveys indicate that managers usually find it no harder to manage a team than to manage an individual on any particular job.

In scheduling job sharers' time, it is necessary not only that work time match job requirements, but also that supervisors and co-workers know each partner's assigned work schedule. Various schedules have been used. Split weeks are most common. Other alternatives include: half-days; one week on, one week off; and, in the case of some civil engineers and probation workers, six months on and six months off. Occasionally, when the work demands, both sharers work at the same time, and full time, until the peak passes. Many schedules overlap so that the sharers may confer together daily or weekly.

J ob sharers need to develop formal communication systems in addition to overlap time, rather than rely on time outside of scheduled hours. Methods include logbooks, notes, staff meetings, and regular telephone calls. A side benefit of the communication process and the recording of information by job sharers is that often the entire office unit is stimulated to review its procedures and thus raise efficiency. The special conditions of job sharing give team members insights that full-timers may lack.

We recommend that employers and unions give heightened attention to the potential for job sharing as a personnel policy which is responsive to changing life-styles and the dual-worker family and is highly adaptable to organizational needs.

recommendation 20

NOTES

1.   The data are for 1977, based on a survey of employers. See Stanley Nollen and Virginia Hider Martin, *Alternative Work Schedules* (New York: AMACOM, a division of American Management Associations, 1978).

2.   Stanley Nollen, *New Work Schedules in Practice: Managing Time in a Changing Society*. Van Nostrand Reinhold/Work in America Institute Series (New York: Van Nostrand Reinhold, 1981).

III.
Broader Policy Issues

5.

Seeking Solutions to Energy and Commuting Problems through New Work Schedules

Experts agree that the problem of energy will worsen in the 1980s. They differ only as to the pace of deterioration, the rate of increase of prices, the likelihood and timing of supply interruptions, and the remedies.

Since transportation accounts for 53 percent of all petroleum consumed in the United States, whatever improves transportation efficiency is likely to reduce energy usage at the same time. We believe that petroleum can be saved in large quantities by new work schedules that encourage employees to switch to more energy-efficient forms of transportation.

Community-wide flexitime programs have shown solid results and exciting potential, which should draw the interest of governmental leaders at federal, state, and local levels throughout the country. Work in America Institute will ensure that this report comes to their attention, so that opportunities for fruitful partnership between cities and private employers will not be missed.

Flexiplace, which proposes to replace commuting with working at—or near—home, is still in its infancy. Although not yet a trend, flexiplace promises to attract more interest in the future.

If the energy supply should be drastically curtailed and quick, nationwide solutions are needed, the federal government is likely to opt for a four-day week, with or without rationing. The compressed workweek has relatively few adherents at present, but changing circumstances, and certain modifications, might make it more popular and useful.

IMPROVING TRANSPORTATION SERVICE AND EFFICIENCY

Daily experience is a reminder that both public transportation and commuting by private automobile fall far short of decent standards for efficiency and service. This is a national problem because of its energy and tax implications. It is also a serious problem for individuals and employers: commuting difficulties impair employee morale and performance, increase absenteeism and tardiness, and burden employers with higher taxes to improve roads, traffic control, and public transit.

However, the stirrings of change are beginning to be felt. In the last few years it has been observed that new work schedules have a favorable impact on commuter transportation. For example, if employees on flexible work hours choose their work starting times and stopping times, they can usually improve commuting arrangements by switching from private automobile to public transportation or from solo driving to car or van pooling. In fact, the first recorded use of flexitime, in Germany, was designed primarily to solve a tough commuting problem. On the other hand, flexitime sometimes disrupts car pools, since all the employees of any given employer no longer have to arrive at the same time.

Clearly, flexiplace reduces the number of commuting trips made and/or the distance traveled (even if employees work at satellite offices rather than at home).

Compressed workweeks allow fewer commuting trips in a week's time, and perhaps a shift of some travel to off-peak hours, although workers may use their cars more for travel, personal business, or entertainment purposes on their extra weekday off.

Beginning as early as 1970, the Port Authority of New York and New Jersey persuaded many employers to stagger the starting times for their employees, in groups (e.g., some at 8:00 a.m. and some at 8:30 a.m.). The success of that program has inspired a growing number of cities to plan or experiment with city-wide flexible-work-hours programs (more than 20 cities were known to be doing so as of 1981).

Several cities have mounted city-wide programs in which a large number of employers in the central business district change from fixed to flexible hours. Federal government pressure to develop local transportation system management plans is also stimulating the consideration of city-wide flexitime.

A large-scale conversion to compressed workweeks took place among federal government employees in Denver in 1979, in part to improve transportation efficiency.

COMMUTING PROBLEMS AND THEIR CAUSES

This report touches only one aspect of transportation—commuting, whether by public or private conveyance, and the ways in which changes in work schedules might affect it.

Commuting to work is beset by three basic problems. The first is excessive commuting time. This problem affects workers and employers, but not public authorities. The second problem is commuting by a disproportionately large number of single drivers in private cars, a practice which wastes energy and causes severe traffic congestion and parking problems. These problems, in turn, put pressure on public agencies to spend more on costly capital-improvement projects, such as roads and parking garages. Single-driver cars are less of a headache for workers and employers (except as they indirectly increase commuting time for all employees) than for public authorities.

The third basic commuting problem is the quality of public transportation, specifically, the massive imbalances between public transportation system costs and revenues, necessitating public subsidies; the low level of efficiency with which capital equipment (buses, railroad cars) and labor are utilized; and the slow, erratic, unreliable service.

The need for commuting is not likely to go away soon. Millions of American workers have to travel long distances from home to work. A long history of economic, social, and technological developments produced this state of affairs. For example, there are economies from having work sites located together in a central business district. Zoning laws enforce the split between work sites and home sites in many cases. Differences in real estate values make it impossible for many workers to live in the central business district even if they wanted to.

Since commuting must take place, fixed work schedules that are virtually identical among many employers cause rush-hour traffic peaks and congestion on roads, railroads, and buses.

Mass transit is unsatisfactory in many cities because of a host of intractable economic and political problems. But poor, inefficient, or unsafe mass transit is shunned by a large proportion of commuters, which only increases commuting by private vehicle and aggravates the problem.

CAN NEW WORK SCHEDULES RELIEVE COMMUTING PROBLEMS?

Do new work schedules help to solve commuting transportation problems? If so, which of them help in solving which kind of transportation problem? How much aid can they provide? In what kinds of cities are they likely to succeed? What contingencies determine the outcome?

New work schedules are only one of many ingredients needed to get at commuting problems, which are, after all, city-wide infrastructure problems. If only a few employers adopt new work schedules, the overall effect will be negligible. For example, flexitime cannot reduce rush-hour congestion nor shorten travel time unless a critical mass of employers adopt it. Public transportation usage cannot increase if the service is not available.

If bridges, tunnels, or buses are already used up to capacity for three-hour periods during morning and afternoon rush hours, neither flexitime nor compressed workweeks will spread the rush-hour peak enough to matter.

A second set of issues concerns the way in which effective new work schedules can be put into place. What roles do private companies take? What initiatives are up to public authorities? For example, how can city-wide flexitime or compressed workweek programs be managed?

Based on the actual experiences of cities and employers across the country, we believe that wider use of some new work schedules can contribute toward easing commuting transportation problems.

Flexitime

Flexitime, when applied on a large scale, can significantly improve transportation efficiency and service and thus save energy. Many cities—Baltimore, Boise, Boston, Chicago, Cleveland, Duluth, Kansas City, Knoxville, Milwaukee, New York City, Ottawa, Pittsburgh, Portland, Richmond, San Francisco, Seattle, Toronto, and Washington, D.C.—are planning or experimenting with area-wide flexitime programs, some in connection with contingency plans developed for the Urban Mass Transportation Administration and the Federal Highway Administration. These programs are attractive because they require no capital investment, they cost far less to operate than it costs to computerize traffic control or expand local bus systems, and they need little government action to keep going once they are under way.

Flexitime spreads commuting peak loads to off-peak periods immediately before and after the rush hour, and thus shortens commuting time. It also improves the match between capacity and load by smoothing and speeding the flow of traffic, which defers or eliminates some of the need for new construction. Shifts away from solo driving and toward car pools, and sometimes toward public transportation, are responsible for these good effects.

One potential disadvantage is that building utility costs may rise if employees arrive earlier and stay later than usual. However, that disadvantage can probably be offset.

Area-wide flexitime experiments of Seattle and Boston are described below. (For further detail, see the casebook for this policy study, *New Work Schedules in Practice*.[1]) In these cases, government and business joined in organized efforts to persuade employers to adopt flexitime for their employees. The early results of two other experiments have also been analyzed.

In Seattle and King County, Washington, the proportion of flexitime employees who commuted during the morning peak hour of 7:30 a.m. to 8:30 a.m. decreased from 75 percent before city-wide flexitime to 42 percent afterwards. These employees began to commute at earlier hours when there was spare capacity on public buses. Travel time was reduced for most of them, with 30 percent saving more than 10 minutes per trip, and 43 percent saving six or more minutes. Commuting shifted to more energy-efficient modes: for example, solo driving decreased from 24 percent to 14 percent of flexitime employees, while ride sharing and public-transit usage both increased.

In Boston, the Massachusetts Bay Transit Authority reported that, two years after a city-wide flexitime program was launched, utilization of public transit had improved; the number of commuters boarding subway cars during rush hour at the four most congested subway stations had diminished by 21 to 46 percent, while those boarding subway cars in the periods immediately before and after the peak period increased. Employees in 12 state agencies that participated in the city-wide flexitime effort saved two hours per week in commuting time on the average, and 83 percent of the employees found commuting easier.

Among state government employees on flexitime, commuting by driving alone decreased from 15 to 8 percent, while public transit use increased from 71 to 77 percent. Car pooling was unaffected, but auto ownership decreased 13 percent.

Similar results were reported in San Francisco and Kansas City. Other programs, in Ottawa, Toronto, and Richmond, Virginia, all succeeded in lessening traffic congestion.

In Ottawa the number of federal employees who started work during the heaviest 30-minute rush-hour peak period dropped from 78 to 40 percent after flexitime was implemented. In Toronto, after a year of city-wide flexitime, almost half of the downtown employees on flexible hours chose to travel outside the peak rush hour in the morning; peak 15-minute subway usage during the morning period was halved.

The consumption of gasoline diminished because (1) time per trip was reduced, and (2) steadier driving resulted in higher mileage per gallon. A small proportion of employees on flexitime changed their mode of travel; those who did so turned mostly toward more energy-efficient forms, such as ride sharing or public transit.

Based on 11 case studies, the percentage of commuters driving alone decreased by one to ten percentage points (about five points, on average) *after* flexitime. The percentage who shared a ride increased by one to twelve percentage points, with the average at three percentage points. The percentage of commuters using mass transit ranged from a decrease of five percentage points to an increase of seventeen percentage points; on average, however, the change was toward more transit usage, by about two percentage points.

Higher gas prices motivated the mode changes; flexitime facilitated them. The Ottawa flexitime program also significantly increased the productivity of buses and their drivers, thereby reducing the need for additional transport resources.

In all the above cities, the proportion of central business district employees on flexitime ranged between 12 and 30 percent.

Rush-hour peaks will remain despite flexible work schedules; demand for bus and train operators will continue to be cyclical over the day. The wage premiums associated with split shifts for full-time operators and the unnecessary costs of idle operators can be minimized by the use of permanent part-time operators. Where collective bargaining agreements prohibit the use of permanent part-time employees, it may be wise for unions to reexamine and relax these prohibitions before an economic crunch compels them to do so. Indeed, new California state legislation declares that a transit system is eligible for state operating subsidies only if collective bargaining agreements permit part-time employment.

The manner and degree to which an area-wide work-rescheduling program can increase energy efficiency depends on several factors, such as population size, transit system density, geography, and industry mix. For example, slight shifts in schedules can improve commuting dramatically in smaller cities, because peak periods there are of shorter duration and program organization is less complex. Similarly, flexitime's utility increases with the distance between residential and working areas. These factors are important, not only on their own merit, but because of their interaction.

When a program is undertaken, it requires cooperation among employers, employees, transit operators, and government officials. The concerns of all these groups must be taken into account to determine the feasibility of an area-wide program.

recommendation 21

State and local governments, in concert with employers and unions, should take the initiative in organizing area-wide flexitime programs. It would be particularly helpful if the governments involved were to adopt flexitime for their own employees.

The experience of pioneering cities with city-wide flexitime shows that success is enhanced (1) if the business sector acknowledges the existence of a transportation problem (perhaps linked with an energy or air-quality problem) and is represented by an influential council; (2) if public transportation and highway agencies facing budgetary stringencies build flexitime into their capital budget and operating plans; (3) if the city has a transportation system management plan for an energy emergency, which includes flexitime; and (4) if political support is visible. For example, if it becomes clear that no more roads are to be built and that the economic prosperity of the central business district is in jeopardy, city-wide flexitime becomes an immediate answer. When San Francisco was recruiting employers into its city-wide flexitime program, one of the most effective approaches was an appeal to help avoid the "Manhattanization" of the city.

In Seattle, business leaders were persuaded to try flexitime by other businessmen who had themselves adopted it successfully.

Local authorities and employers should give preference to city-wide flexitime programs over staggered hours as a progressive transportation management strategy.

recommendation 22

Flexitime does everything that a staggered-hours program does, and more, without the drawbacks of staggered hours. The key advantage of flexitime is that each worker has a much wider range of options for transportation. The evidence so far is that workers on flexitime typically advance their starting hours by more than most employers would dare to require in a staggered-hours arrangement. Thus the rush "hour" extends over a longer period of time. Furthermore, flexitime takes less central administration, since most decisions are transferred to the level of local work units.

While staggered hours will force some equalization of commuting traffic flows, the scheme does not permit workers to achieve better matches, day in, day out, between their schedules and public transportation or carpool schedules. The only advantage staggered hours have over flexitime is that they appear to employers to be a less radical change and hence are more quickly embraced. However, as the popularity of flexitime spreads, this advantage will fade.

As a means of strengthening the impact of an area-wide flexitime program:

a. Mass-transit operators should adopt pricing and marketing strategies that enhance the value of flexitime, for example, by offering, as some cities now do, free or low-cost rides during off-peak hours.

recommendation 23

b. Employers and governments should encourage car and van pooling, for example, by computer matching of sharers, by offering incentives (such as direct payments, use of pooled vans for nonwork life, and preferential or inexpensive parking), by granting social recognition, and by creating priority lanes.

Medium-sized cities and suburban employment centers are likely to experience noticeable benefits from flexitime, primarily because their rush-hour peak periods are usually of shorter duration than those of large cities, and their road and public transportation systems are less likely to be operating above capacity for more than brief periods. City-wide flexitime works best when the transportation problem is of manageable proportions. Even if public transportation systems are not very dense, city-wide flexitime will encourage ride sharing and improve transportation efficiency. Indeed, medium-sized and suburban work sites traditionally encourage solo driving more than metropolitan areas do, and that is the mode most frequently diminished. While obvious traffic bottlenecks, such as bridges and tunnels, usually precipitate city-wide programs, rush-hour congestion, whatever the cause, will be eased by city-wide flexitime.

recommendation 24

Local authorities and employers in small and medium-sized cities should adopt city-wide flexitime programs, whether or not there are obvious traffic bottlenecks or inadequate public-transportation systems.

To what extent are the transportation savings achieved by means of flexitime or staggered hours offset by increased energy consumption in the facilities where the employees work? The answer varies from case to case. In many buildings flexitime and staggered hours would have no appreciable effect. In such facilities, for example, lights, heating, and cooling systems operate 24 hours a day anyway.

Many buildings can be retrofitted to make their insulation more effective. Where this is properly done, the need for heating and cooling can be greatly reduced and the energy increment due to earlier starts and later finishes would be negligible. Other offsets could be gained through the use of more suitable clothing, window fans during early and late hours of the summer, openable instead of fixed windows, and other such methods.

Another major energy cost is associated with the fact that most workplaces open and close at the same hours. Peak loading of residential energy use, which requires more generating capacity, corresponds with the beginning and ending of the workday. Many summer brownouts, for example, occur when masses of employees return home from work at the same time and turn on their air conditioners. Flexitime and staggered hours, by spreading the hours of leaving and returning, can reduce peak loads enough to avert the need for additional capacity.

recommendation 25

State and local governments, regulatory agencies, and public utilities should join in promoting area-wide flexitime and should make it more attractive with price structures that favor use of electricity at nonpeak hours. California's program of low-cost loans by utilities to homeowners, which has helped keep prices down by making additional capacity unnecessary, is a good analogy.

Part-Time Work

The impact of part-time work on energy usage is extremely variable. If people work every day, but only part of the day, the impact depends on (1) whether employees are at the workplace during the hours when energy is being used anyway, and (2) whether mass transit, or car or van pooling, is available at times of the day when needed. However, if people work full days, but less than five full days a week, the impact is neutral. And if part-time work enables people to work at home, commuting is eliminated entirely.

Flexiplace

Frank Schiff, vice-president and chief economist of the Committee for Economic Development and a member of the advisory board for this policy study, has raised more basic issues about saving the energy now consumed in commuting to work:

- How much present-day commuting is actually necessary?
- How many jobs or tasks can be done just as efficiently and effectively at home, or in a nearby satellite building, as at the present place of work?
- To what extent can telecommunications replace the physical movement of people to and from work?

(The general advantages of flexiplace to employers and employees have been reviewed in chapter 3, "Choosing New Work Schedules.")

It is not necessary to urge that people work at home or at the satellite location *all* the time. For employees on a five-day week, each day free of commuting represents a 20 percent energy saving for the week (not to mention the saving of their own personal time on the road). The question is, how many commuters could—and how many would, if they could—do their work at home?

The telecommunications systems and equipment to permit flexiplace are already available: computer terminals, long-distance dictating equipment, microfiche, electric typewriters, computerized drafting machines. Transferability of work between the central workplace and home is most apparent in the case of office work, and office workers comprise a very large part of the commuting population. On the other hand, it should not be taken for granted that blue-collar work can be done only at the central workplace.

The original reason for separating the work site from the home during the Industrial Revolution was the need for a central power source to operate heavy machinery. It seems logical, then, that today's technology could be the moving force in transferring many jobs back to the home, away from a central plant or office. Zoning laws that separate industrial and commercial uses from residential often enshrine out-of-date conceptions of factory and office conditions. To the extent that they preclude the dispersal of satellite offices or plants closer to workers' homes, and thus discourage the transportation savings that would come from flexiplace, these zoning restrictions ought to be changed.

Several companies in this country, large and small, are beginning to experiment with flexiplace (e.g., Control Data Corporation's "home-work" program, and Continental Illinois Bank's satellite offices).

Several questions remain before flexiplace can be widely recommended. Will the use of homes as offices by employees cause problems with actual or attempted tax deductions? Can the performance of employees be appraised adequately if they are seldom in an office or plant and supervisors cannot see whether they are at work? Will companies save money because less office or plant space is required, or will overhead costs rise due to equipment being relocated in employees' homes? Will the work effectiveness of some employees who work at home be impaired by the disruptions of household activities? How widespread is the applicability of flexiplace?

recommendation
26

Since the advantages of flexiplace would accrue even more to society than to employers, the federal government and major foundations should sponsor large-scale pilot studies on the technical feasibility of flexiplace, not only in government employment, but also in private employment. Private employers should also introduce such pilot studies.

Emergency Solutions

Any serious discussion of work schedules and energy must consider what to do in the event of a shutoff or drastic reduction of the supply of foreign oil. In a recent Conference Board survey, 52 percent of the public declared that they preferred rationing, even under nonemergency conditions, rather than increases in the price of fuel. Also the average family in that survey estimated that it could reduce driving by 11 percent, a saving of 200 million barrels of gasoline a year. Rationing would also create strong incentives to buy smaller cars, to pool cars, to use public transit, and to plan trips more carefully.

The work schedule which most effectively reduces the amount of fuel used in commuting is the compressed workweek. Although numerous forms of compressed workweeks have been tested, the one most readily applicable to the largest number of employers would be the workweek of four 10-hour days. Since 6 million barrels of gasoline are consumed per day, a 20 percent reduction in commuting would save 1.2 million barrels per day.

There is some debate as to whether the savings due to not commuting on the fifth day would be offset by increased nonwork use of the automobile.

Recent case-study evidence of a large-scale compressed workweek experiment among federal employees in Denver is encouraging. These compressed workweek employees (equal numbers of whom were on a four-day workweek and on the 5/4-9 plan) experienced a 15 percent reduction in the average vehicle miles traveled per week to and from work. But they also showed a similar decrease in total miles traveled per week for *all* purposes. Apparently, they shifted some weekend personal travel to their extra weekday off, and they did less personal driving in connection with commuting trips. (In Ottawa, Canada, however, there was an increase in personal travel on the extra weekday off.) In Denver, on Tuesdays through Thursdays, the number of compressed workweek employees arriving at work during the peak one-half hour rush periods was reduced by 25 percent within the central business district and by 10 percent outside the central business district. Commuting time per day was reduced by 14 percent. No significant changes in commuting mode took place: although employees on compressed schedules tended to do more ride sharing, employees not on compressed schedules in the same agencies found some disruption of their ride-sharing arrangements.

A feature that makes the compressed week unattractive to many workers is the combination of commuting time plus ten-hour days. This disadvantage may fade as energy problems intensify and workers seek larger blocks of free time. It may become feasible for Congress to legislate the 36-hour week composed of four nine-hour days, whereby society would gain fuel conservation without public anger, employees would gain increased leisure and family time without undue fatigue at work, and the unions would achieve their long-sought goal of the shorter workweek without reduced pay. Indeed, the trend among compressed-week experiments in the federal government is toward nine-hour days in the 5/4-9 plan.

Large-scale adoption of compressed workweeks would also remove the feeling of being out of step with the rest of the world. Service industries, such as banking and retailing, could level out their work load by going on to a seven-day week, with two work forces for coverage. Other industries could operate four, five, or six days a week, as needed, although some interesting problems of holiday or weekend premiums might arise.

Central cities, where service firms predominate, might be made more accessible for leisure use on the three-day weekends. Public schools might also go on a four-day basis, which would save 20 percent of the fuel used by school buses and parents' cars.

Even without rationing, it is conceivable that if gasoline prices were to reach European levels, the government might enact the four-day workweek.

The rigors of the compressed workweek could also be relaxed by breaking up the week. For example, instead of working four successive ten-hour days, employees might prefer to work two days, take off the third, work the next two, and then have the normal two-day weekend rather than a three-day weekend.

recommendation 27

We recommend that if at some future time gasoline rationing goes into effect, Congress should enact the four-day workweek simultaneously, with each driver's ration based on a 20 percent reduction of commuting travel and no increase in noncommuting travel.

recommendation 28

Every organization should develop and keep up to date a contingency plan under which its employees work a four-day week, even if the workplace itself has to remain open five, six, or seven days a week.

recommendation 29

Since commuting adds to the unattractiveness of ten-hour days, employers operating on the compressed workweek should, whenever practical, also adopt flexitime or staggered hours, which not only ease commuting but save energy in their own right.

As pointed out, the workweek of four 10-hour days is unattractive to many employees. The prospect of gradual shortening of the workday without loss of pay would help relieve some of the discontent.

recommendation 30

If it should become necessary to maintain the four-day week, Congress should legislate a 36-hour workweek, i.e., a week of four nine-hour days, reducing the traditional 40-hour workweek by one hour a week each year over a period of four years, with no loss in pay.

This 2.5 percent per year reduction in hours would require an offsetting 2.5 percent increase in productivity, which could be achieved through tighter management, higher morale, reduced absenteeism and turnover, and the good effects of increased leisure time.

Alternatively, the work time lost due to the shorter workweek might be partially traded off against a reduction in the number of paid holidays. For example, the loss of 200 hours of labor time per year could be half recovered if ten holidays were given back. Since most holidays are celebrated on Mondays or Fridays, the loss might be acceptable in exchange for three-day weekends every weekend, more time off from work, and no loss of pay.

The new workweek proposed would realize a long-standing wish of organized labor for a shorter workweek. For management, this gain by labor might take the pressure off future negotiations and contribute to better industrial relations.

Further offsets might be created by moderation in energy prices, stemming from the decreased demand for commuting energy and other national economic gains that would flow indirectly from more efficient utilization of social institutions.

NOTES

1. Stanley Nollen, *New Work Schedules in Practice: Managing Time in a Changing Society*, Van Nostrand Reinhold/Work in America Institute Series (New York: Van Nostrand Reinhold, 1981).

6.

New Work Schedules and Employment Policy

WORK SHARING

New work schedules have yet to find their rightful place in the field of employment policy. Work sharing, part-time employment, and job sharing hold great promise for job security, job creation, and expansion of the labor supply. Congress has already begun to consider this issue, but public understanding lags far behind.

Layoffs are the standard reaction of American employers to serious downturns in business. Their impact on individuals, families, businesses, communities, the economy, and politics is destructive and pervasive. Work sharing is the practice of averting layoffs by reducing the number of hours of work, and wages in proportion, for the entire work force or occupational segment, instead of compelling part of the work force to bear the entire burden.

Since 1949 the United States has experienced seven recessions, and the underlying rate of unemployment has risen from 4 percent to almost 8 percent. Individual industries and firms have had their ups and downs within this pattern.

Each time large-scale layoffs occur, society undergoes severe shocks:

☐ Laid-off workers suffer loss of wages, benefits, security, morale, skills, work habits, and physical and psychic health. Many remaining workers are "bumped" into lower-paid jobs.

☐ Family ties are strained—offset, in part, by the fact that more families now have multiple wage earners.

☐ Payments on mortgages and cars are not met.

☐ Layoffs hurt the employer, too. Productivity is lost due to the reworking of production schedules and the "bumping" of workers. Unemployment insurance premiums increase.

☐ Violence and crimes increase.

☐ Each 1 percent increase in unemployment is reflected in a 2 percent increase in the mortality rate within five years.

☐ Communities take on heavier costs for health, welfare, police, and other services, while revenues diminish.

☐ Each 1 percent increase of unemployment costs the federal government $20 billion of benefit payments and lost revenues.

☐ Unemployment insurance and Social Security funds are drained.

☐ The federal budget moves further into deficit, and government is pressed to take measures that permanently distort the economy.

In most cases, especially where employees are unionized, the order of layoff and recall is determined by length of service or seniority under the principle of last in, first out. Women, youth, and members of minority groups make up a disproportionate share of the victims. Many cannot afford to wait to be recalled, so they seek jobs elsewhere, begin again with zero seniority, and remain permanently vulnerable.

The chief impediment to work sharing lies in the rigidity of the unemployment insurance system. If this impediment could be removed and if large numbers of employers and employees were to adopt work sharing in place of layoffs, many advantages would flow:

Advantages to Employers

1. Maintenance of productivity because of higher morale and preservation of employee skills.

2. Retention of skilled workers.

3. Reduction or elimination of the large costs associated with layoffs, particularly where "bumping" occurs, for example, distorted production scheduling, delayed start-ups when recession ends, retraining of bumped employees.

4. Greater flexibility in deploying human resources to keep operations going.

5. Savings in employer costs associated with severance pay, early-retirement incentives, and other layoff schemes requiring substantial financing.

6. Avoidance of post-recession costs of hiring and training new workers to replace those who found other jobs during layoff.

7. Reinforcing group loyalties and strengthening employee loyalty to the firm.

Advantages to Workers

1. Continued job attachment for workers who would otherwise have been laid off.

2. Continued fringe-benefit protection for employees and their families.

3. Retention of more minority and women workers, thus preserving the aims and achievements of affirmative action.

4. Security for older workers, who cost more, are often among the first fired in selective layoffs, and are discriminated against when they seek new jobs.

5. Opportunity for workers with high seniority to trade work for increased leisure, with only a small decrease in take-home pay, thus providing a "taste" of retirement without fear of unemployment.

6. More effective preservation of the family income of two-paycheck families than if one member continues to work full time and the other is on unemployment insurance, particularly if the wife is a new entry into the labor force. (Women's traditional jobs are generally low paying, and eligibility rules for unemployment insurance require workers to meet a combination of dollar amount and time in covered occupations. For some new entrants, these benefits may be low or nonexistent.)

Advantages to Unions

1. Preservation of union membership and members' ability and willingness to pay dues.

2. Greater ability to take into account diverse interests of membership and fairly represent all employees in the bargaining unit.

3. Improved long-run prospects for the union. Layoffs generally pose problems for unions because some laid-off workers do not return, new employees have to be organized, and returning workers may have less enthusiasm for the union after extended unemployment.

4. Less polarization between groups represented by the union.

5. Increased support from new workers who would otherwise be laid off.

6. Greater bargaining flexibility when an employer suffers a downturn.

Advantages to Society

1. Protection of affirmative action and equal employment opportunity advances.

2. Less need for public-service jobs.

3. Less need for public assistance for the unemployed.

4. No increase in net unemployment insurance costs.

5. Less disruption of the society as a whole.

Sharing the available work can take many forms, depending on the nature of the organization and its productive processes. The most common is reduction of the workweek, usually from five days to four. Other options include reducing the hours of work per day, shutting down the entire plant for a week or more, and alternating or rotating layoffs. In the latter arrangement, part of the work force is laid off for a period, after which it returns to work, and another group is laid off for a similar period.

Union Contracts for Reduced Work Hours—without U.I. Compensation

The principle of work sharing is as old as cottage industries.

A number of unions, acting from historical principles of solidarity, do negotiate collective bargaining agreements calling for a reduction in hours or a sharing of work among employees before layoffs are permitted. Work sharing is also seen as a plus by some nonunion employers, such as Lincoln Electric, which has avoided layoffs for over 35 years.

Collective bargaining provisions which require or permit various kinds of work sharing are spread across a wide variety of manufacturing and nonmanufacturing industries. While some contracts call for mandatory division of available work, generally the use of work sharing is permissive. About one-third of the major contracts surveyed by the Bureau of Labor Statistics contain permissive clauses allowing reduction in hours, often up to one day a week, in place of layoffs.[1] However, in only a few industries is work sharing systematically practiced.

Where there is a union, the subject of work sharing or layoff is a mandatory subject for collective bargaining. Since the 1975-76 recession, a new section heading for "work sharing, to avoid layoff" has been added to the index of *Labor Arbitration Reports*, indicating increased use of this technique.

Division-of-work clauses predominate in the apparel industry as a means of handling the variation in work loads which have always been part of the industry's operation. Procedures are generally worked out at the local level by the local union representative and the employer. In some cases, work sharing takes the form of a shorter workweek for all employees. In other cases, where the reduction in work load is more serious, work sharing can take the form of alternate weeks of employment for the regular employees. In particularly difficult circumstances, layoffs do occur.

Reduction-in-hour clauses are found in many of the Bell Telephone System agreements with the Communication Workers of America and the International Brotherhood of Electrical Workers. In the steel industry, contracts with the Steelworkers provide local options to reduce work to 32 hours a week. Many construction industry unions, as well as the Graphic Arts and Teamsters unions, have also utilized forms of work sharing.

In 1974, the American Newspaper Guild signed an agreement with the *Washington Star* for a four-day week with a 20 percent reduction in salary as an alternative to layoff.

More recently, a union faced with a painful problem developed an inventive solution that may have wider applicability to other companies and industries. In the 1980 recession, United Airlines found it necessary to lay off 200 flight attendants. The Association of Flight Attendants agreed that economic conditions warranted belt tightening, but it rejected management's proposal. It made a counteroffer of a program of voluntary job sharing, which the company accepted. Two-hundred-and-fifty attendants volunteered to form job-sharing teams. In most cases, a team consisted of one fairly junior and one fairly senior employee, thus spreading the burden more equitably. The job sharers agreed in writing to ensure that all assignments were properly covered and to work out by themselves the details of pay, benefits, and hours of work. Thus 125 out of 200 proposed layoffs were averted.

Another example of work sharing is the system of voluntary furloughs developed by TWA and its flight attendants to cope with the slack periods that occur twice every year. Employees take leave without pay, but their fringe benefits continue in effect.

Although the principle is widespread, unions seldom invoke contractual rights to share work. A principal reason is that unemployment insurance laws and regulations are biased, not without justification, against partial layoffs. Work sharing has, in fact, fallen off since the introduction of unemployment insurance.

Unemployment Insurance Laws as Obstacle

Under the current system an organization whose production schedule requires it to reduce labor hours by 20 percent has, in theory, two options. It can lay off 20 percent of the work force, whereupon the remaining 80 percent continue working full time and the 20 percent laid off become eligible for unemployment compensation, without administrative fuss. Alternatively, the organization can reduce everyone's work hours and pay by 20 percent. Should it do so by having them work four eight-hour days a week and take the fifth day off, unemployment compensation would probably not be paid for that fifth day. Although most states allow partial benefits for days lost in this manner, the formulas for computing benefits are so stringent as to be useless for work sharing, except in California.

Generally, the benefit payable for part-week unemployment is reckoned as the benefit for a full week of unemployment minus wages earned during the week. Anyone whose earnings exceed the weekly maximum benefit is thus ineligible for benefits, even if unemployed for most of the week. Some employers, exploiting these provisions, schedule enough work each week so that employees earn just over the unemployment insurance limit, and *then* they lay them off for the rest of the week. Thus employees are barred from collecting compensation, and the employer's experience-rated payroll tax is held down.

The basic federal-state unemployment insurance system is financed by employer taxes. Each employer's tax depends in part on the employer's layoff record. Extensive layoffs increase the employer's tax rate unless the maximum has already been reached.

Some states raise additional legal impediments, such as waiting periods, that make less-than-full-week unemployment impracticable. Where work sharing is used consistently, whether in union or nonunion shops, unemployment schedules may be keyed into local compensation requirements. For example, to avoid waiting-period requirements and maximum weekly pay limits, employees might work alternate weeks, thus becoming eligible to collect for their downtime.

In the absence of a short-time unemployment compensation (STC) program, it may nevertheless be possible to achieve the desired results by means of layoff rotation. For example, in 1975 the Tomkins-Johnson Company, with plants in Michigan, Oregon, and Alabama, responded to the deep recession by putting 160 blue-collar (nonunion) employees on a rotation plan. For a period of four months, each employee worked four weeks and was laid off for the fifth week. This reduced each individual's work time by 20 percent, just as a four-day workweek would have done. The state paid full unemployment benefits for every fifth week.

The scheme was feasible because two of the states had no waiting period for benefits and one had a one-week waiting period, and because only the most junior production, maintenance, and technical employees—those whose base wages averaged only $30-$35 more than the maximum weekly unemployment benefit for which they were eligible—were rotated. Yet, had they claimed benefits for one day's layoff per week, they would have received nothing at all.

Reactions to the program, tested by means of attitude surveys, were highly favorable—so favorable that when it became necessary to reduce work time for secretarial, engineering, and customer-service employees in the 1980 slowdown, the same plan was put into effect.

A number of other employers, including some organized by the United Steelworkers and by the Amalgamated Clothing and Textile Workers, have also used layoff rotation successfully.

Short-Time Unemployment Compensation
Legislation—the West German Model

In the United States, California is the first state to have passed a law especially adapted to short-time unemployment compensation (STC). (Arizona recently enacted similar legislation.) California modeled its statute on West Germany's, although many other countries—Belgium, France, Italy, Great Britain, Luxembourg, Denmark, the Netherlands, Norway, Australia, and Canada—also have STC laws. The West German plan has been in operation almost 60 years and is considered the most successful of all.

During the 1974-75 recession, 770,000 German workers were on STC, reducing the overall unemployment rate by approximately one percentage point. During the current recession, over half a million employees are drawing STC benefits.

A West German firm becomes eligible for STC by demonstrating that a reduction in hours of labor is unavoidable and that work-time reductions with STC will prevent dismissals. The employer must also document that work-time reductions of at least 10 percent have already been made for at least one-third of their employees, for a period of four continuous weeks. Firms and industries judged to be in permanent decline rather than in temporary recession are usually denied eligibility.

Decisions to reduce work time (or lay workers off) must be reached by agreement between the employer and the works council (which represents all strata of employees, union and nonunion). If the works council consents, the program becomes binding upon all affected workers. Dissenting workers can avoid the shorter workweek only by resigning.

Benefits are paid directly by the firm to its employees, and the government reimburses the firm. The benefits have a ceiling but are free of tax, so that take-home earnings are maintained at 80 to 90 percent of regular earnings. The firm must provide fringe benefits throughout. Normally STC can be drawn for up to six months, but the period can be extended for as much as two years. The typical STC recipient undergoes a work-time reduction of about 40 percent (two days a week) and draws benefits less than three months.

The West German program must be viewed in perspective. European restraints on layoff are much tougher than in the United States. Large parts of European fringe-benefit programs are administered by the government, which reduces the fixed costs of labor. Finally, unemployment-benefit ceilings are considerably higher than those of most American states.[2]

The California Law

The first state program for STC in the United States was adopted by California in 1978, a month before the passage of Proposition 13. The program was given a one-year trial and then extended in 1979 for a second year.

California's program offers partial benefits for up to 20 weeks a year, to workers whose companies put them on short time in order to avoid a layoff. Benefits are proportional to regular unemployment insurance benefits. For example, a worker who would be entitled to $100 for a full week of unemployment would receive $20 for being unemployed one day a week. Since unemployment insurance benefits are tax free and the worker is freed of job-related costs, such as transportation and lunch, most work sharers in California end up with about 90 percent of take-home pay.

Both the firm and its workers have to meet regular California unemployment insurance eligibility requirements.

The employer must state in writing that the firm wishes to participate, declaring that a reduction of work hours in all or part of the establishment is necessary to avoid a layoff. Normal work hours must be reduced at least 10 percent a week for at least 10 percent of the regular permanent work force in the affected unit or units. If employees are represented by a union, the union must consent to the plan. The employer may or may not continue fringe benefits. If participating workers moonlight or work in excess of the planned work time, the extra earnings are deducted from their short-time compensation (STC) benefits.

Workers on STC remain eligible for regular unemployment insurance benefits if they are subsequently laid off. However, the total of short-time compensation and regular benefits per year cannot exceed what they would have been entitled to under regular unemployment insurance.

Employers with a history of heavy use of layoffs, who are already paying maximum tax under the regular unemployment insurance program, must pay a penalty tax in order to participate in STC. A number of firms have made use of STC despite this extra cost.

If an employer states that the shared-work plan will run less than ten weeks, the firm's employees are exempt from the normal requirement to search for work. If, on the other hand, the employer foresees a permanent reduction of the work force, STC beneficiaries must search for work as under the regular unemployment insurance system.[3]

Between July 1978 and September 1980 over 1,290 employer plans, covering 35,300 employees, were approved. Some 16,280 claims were paid, and claimants received payment, on average, for one day's employment per week, for a period of five weeks.

Twelve percent of the plans included employees covered by a collective bargaining agreement, and 22 percent of all employees approved for participation in the program worked for unionized employers.[4]

A limited telephone survey in December 1979 found generally favorable reactions. Of 30 employers who had used the program, 25 favored it strongly; 5 were neutral. Those favoring the program asserted that it helped them retain valued employees, was generally appreciated by employees, and was easy and flexible to administer. Twenty representatives of participating local unions also responded; of these, 14 favored the program, 3 were neutral or unaware, and 3 had not actually been involved. Advantages cited for the program were that work sharing is more equitable than layoffs, that workers are better off financially, and that fringe benefits are maintained (although the employer is not required to do so by law). Four unions had encountered resistance at first, which gradually diminished.[5]

recommendation
31

The results of the California short-time compensation program for work sharing, inconclusive as they are, are good enough to warrant comparable experiments by other states. (Arizona recently passed such a law and New York, Oregon, and possibly others, are considering one.) *Active federal encouragement, advice, and (small amounts of) money would speed the process.*

A bill to accomplish those ends was introduced in the 96th Congress by Representative Patricia Schroeder of Colorado and reintroduced in the 97th.

The bill encourages states to enact laws to provide unemployment benefits to partially unemployed workers. It authorizes the secretary of labor to develop model legislation and to make grants and provide technical assistance to states for developing, enacting, and implementing short-time compensation programs.

States that desire such assistance must apply for it, and their short-time compensation programs must conform to the guidelines in the legislation and in regulations to be promulgated by the secretary of labor.

The guidelines for the programs are as follows:

☐ An individual whose workweek has been reduced by at least 10 percent would be eligible for a *pro rata* portion of the unemployment benefits to which he or she would be entitled if totally laid off. Those who object to short-time compensation would be free to quit and receive regular unemployment compensation.

☐ Benefits would be financed by employers through the usual manner of charging reserve accounts by experience rating. However, employers with negative-reserve accounts may be required by the states to pay a surtax or make full reimbursement to the trust fund at the end of the year for benefits charged against their reserve accounts.

☐ Employers must certify that the reduction in work hours is in lieu of total layoffs, which would result in an equivalent reduction in work hours. They must also certify that employees on short-time compensation will retain health-insurance benefits and pension credits.

☐ In the case of employees represented by a union, the appropriate official of a union (or union hall) must consent to the employer's plan.

The legislation also authorizes the secretary of labor to conduct demonstration projects.

The bill has been criticized on the following grounds:

1. It will lead to speed-ups.

2. It will encourage firms to reduce employment.
3. It will subsidize certain firms.
4. It will force workers in nonunion firms to go on STC.
5. It will not require employers to prove the need for STC.

The first two criticisms imply that STC will enable employers, without loss of production, to cut the work hours of workers whom they have no other way of shedding. In fact, nothing at present can prevent employers from laying off unneeded workers if they want to do so, and layoffs are less expensive and time-consuming than STC.

The third criticism overlooks three points in the bill: (a) tax penalties are imposed on employers who overuse the program; (b) STC is paid to employees, not to employers; and (c) STC is paid only for days not worked, unlike a tax credit, which is paid to employers to reduce their labor costs. It would subsidize employers only if they were somehow barred from laying off their employees.

On the fourth point, it is true that workers not represented by a union would be unable to vote on the employer's proposal to go on STC. However, the bill gives them the option to quit and receive regular unemployment insurance.

The fifth point is correct, but it applies with equal force to employers who lay their employees off.

The AFL-CIO raised two objections to the bill, which have now been met to its satisfaction: (1) the financial solvency of the state employment funds, which seemed to be threatened, will be protected by means of several cost controls; and (2) to prevent employers from laying off short-service employees and then using STC to retain those who are harder to replace, employers will have to certify that no layoffs occurred during the previous four months in units affected by the plan. With these changes, the AFL-CIO now believes STC will offer an attractive bargaining option in place of layoffs.

Congress should enact a short-time compensation (STC) law embodying the key provisions of the Schroeder bill: the development of model STC legislation, and grants and technical assistance to states to assist them in developing, enacting, and implementing STC programs.

recommendation 32

Employers should (1) encourage Congress to pass an STC law embodying the key provisions of the Schroeder bill, and (2) experiment with work sharing as a practical alternative to layoffs.

recommendation 33

recommendation

34

Congress should also consider STC as part of a national anti-recession employment policy and as a possible substitute for some current measures.

STC can be used as a partial substitute for public-works employment programs and for the Trade Adjustment Assistance Act; it can help in making gradual adjustment to the loss of jobs due to technological change, with workers using their days of unemployment to search for new jobs; and it can facilitate skill training.

PART-TIME EMPLOYMENT AND JOB SHARING

In 1980 almost 14 percent of all nonagricultural workers were voluntarily working part time (a total of 11,853,000). Another 9 percent (7,901,000) were working part time involuntarily.

The percentage of voluntary part-time workers rose steadily from 8 percent in 1954 to 14 percent in 1972. Since then it has fluctuated narrowly around 14 percent.

Within these overall figures there is a great variance in the incidence of voluntary part-time work as between men, where it hovers around 7.5 percent, and women, where it is around 22 percent. The rate for men has changed little since 1965. The rate for women was 21 percent in 1965, rose gradually to 24 percent in 1972, and has since declined to 22 percent. Do these trends indicate that the proportion of workers seeking voluntary part-time jobs has leveled off? Or that the number of suitable jobs available has leveled off?

We believe that if suitable jobs were to be had, the number of voluntary part-timers would increase dramatically. A Louis Harris survey of the U.S. work force in 1978 reported that between 30 and 40 million workers said they would trade part of their current income for equivalent free time. If only 20 million agreed to trade 10 percent of their work time in this way, the equivalent of 2,000,000 full-time jobs would be created.[6]

□ It is clear that many people would like to job share, if they could—for example, women entering the work force for the first time, women re-entering the work force, single heads of households, older people, and young people with strong professional qualifications.

□ The National Center for Education estimates that of the 13.5 million college graduates who will enter the work force during the 1980s, 2.3 million will not find openings in the occupations for which they prepared. The Bureau of Labor Statistics predicts that one in four will have to take a job that does not require a college degree. Very likely, many of these graduates would prefer shared jobs at work of their own choice, rather than full-time jobs that do not challenge them.

☐ Part-time work is a preferred solution for young people who are trying to complete their education, especially in community colleges, before settling into a permanent career.

☐ According to the BLS, 60 percent of working women work for economic reasons: they are single, widowed, divorced, separated, or married to husbands who earn less than $10,000 a year. Among older women, the percentage is even higher. Currently almost 15 percent of American families are headed by women. Good part-time jobs would facilitate their efforts to combine economic and familial responsibilities.

☐ Increased employment of older workers would greatly reduce the drain on the Social Security fund. In May 1977, 39 percent of employed men over age 65 and 54 percent of employed women over 65 worked part time. With inflation has come a growing need for the elderly to supplement retirement benefits with part-time paid work. According to the Louis Harris poll of 1978, 51 percent of older workers—both those who are retired and those who are not—would like to work beyond age 65, and the majority would prefer part-time to full-time jobs.[7]

In a recent survey, Travelers Insurance Company found that 15 percent of its employees aged 55-60 planned to work beyond age 65; 22 percent of employees aged 61-62 and 43 percent of employees aged 62-65 also planned to continue working after age 65. A full 85 percent of those surveyed said they wanted part-time jobs. (The company has since taken action to gratify that desire.)

In a pilot survey of 266 older employees of Lockheed/California and of the City of Los Angeles, half of them indicated interest in extending their working lives by means of part-time work, flexitime, job modification, or job transfer (part-time work was the most preferred), provided they were not forced to take a cut in base pay or forgo drawing at least part of their pension. Most of those favoring part-time work wanted to work fewer days per week rather than fewer hours per day.[8]

(Managers, on the other hand, regarded part-time work as primarily a means of meeting peak demands, and therefore preferred the part-year variety. Union leaders who represented the interviewees were unaware of these attitudes on the part of their members and did not support part-time jobs.[9])

Many workers presently employed full time would probably convert to part-time work under the right conditions. In the federal part-time program, for instance, over 20 percent of the new part-time jobs were filled by people previously working full time. Other examples of part-time programs follow:

☐ When Wisconsin's Project JOIN was initiated in 1976 to test the concept of job sharing in professional and paraprofessional positions, 65 percent of those who became job sharers were previous full-time state employees who voluntarily took this opportunity to reduce their work hours.

☐ A survey of the Wisconsin civil service indicated that 6 percent of the state's full-time employees were willing to reduce their workweek with a corresponding reduction in pay.

☐ A survey in Minnesota indicated that 13 percent of full-time state employees were interested in working a 20-hour week, while 19 percent expressed interest in a 30-hour workweek.

☐ In Santa Clara County, California, 17 percent of the county employees said they would accept a voluntary reduction in pay for a commensurate amount of time off. Fifteen percent of those who were offered the opportunity, accepted it, taking an average reduction of 10 percent.[10]

☐ When the DuPont Company in Athens, Georgia, wanted to keep its textile-fiber packaging plant in operation for seven days a week, and its regular full-time work force refused to work weekends, DuPont brought in a whole new weekend work force—students from the University of Georgia, housewives, single mothers, a few farmers, and townspeople who needed extra cash. The weekend work force actually ran the plant on the weekends and were paid the same salaries as regular workers. They dispelled any doubts that part-timers were not reliable and would not be able to maintain a good safety record.[11]

☐ BLS statistics show a growing interest in longer vacations in lieu of higher salaries. In spite of increased growth in paid vacations, between 1968 and 1979, those favoring an additional full week of vacation *without pay* rose from 14 percent to 20 percent for men, and from 34 percent to 39 percent for women.[12]

Recognizing society's interest in encouraging part-time employment, the federal government and at least ten state governments have passed legislation or set up programs to open new jobs in government for part-timers and job sharers. California and Wisconsin have the most intensive programs.

The public sector has been interested in work-time alternatives for several reasons:

■ To manage human resources more efficiently.

■ To increase affirmative-action hiring at entry level and in higher positions.

■ To add to the attractions of jobs currently subject to high turnover.

■ To retain valued employees.

- To maintain quality programs and extend services.
- To counter "burnout," which diminishes employee productivity in certain jobs. Part-time social workers, probation officers, teachers, librarians, public-assistance lawyers, and mental-health workers were found to have higher productivity, less stress, and greater job satisfaction than full-time workers in those jobs.
- To encourage new entrants into tenure systems like teaching, while retaining older personnel who wish to reduce their work hours. This has the added advantage of saving money by pairing people from the higher and lower ends of the salary scale. Interest has grown as cost cuts compel a search for more efficient ways to maintain service.

The Federal Employees Part-Time Career Opportunity Act, passed by the 95th Congress, established a uniform part-time hiring policy for the federal government. It requires agencies to expand permanent part-time career positions in grade levels GS-1 to GS-15 by setting annual goals and timetables for hiring. It requires permanent part-timers to be paid at the same wage rate as full-time workers and to receive prorated fringe benefits. And for purposes of the Office of Management and Budget's agency personnel ceilings, it requires part-timers to be counted by full-time equivalents (FTEs), based on the fraction of the 40-hour week worked.

Although most of the jobs are still in the lower grade levels, in 1979-80 about 6,000 of the 20,000 part-timers hired in federal agencies were above the GS-5 level, and about 1,200 were above GS-11.

Perceptions of part-time employment have been generally positive among federal managers, particularly those who had previously used part-timers in their organizations. However, some supervisors fear that identifying a position as suitable for part time would mean the permanent loss of a full-time position and that use of part-timers diminishes the stature of the office.

Currently, 10 states—Alaska, California, Colorado, Hawaii, Massachusetts, Maryland, New York, Oregon, Washington, and Wisconsin—have officially encouraged the use of permanent part-time employment by passing legislation, issuing executive orders, or supporting pilot projects designed to test their feasibility.

In 1978 an amendment to CETA authorized the secretary of labor to undertake research on the applicability of job sharing, work sharing, and other flexible-hours arrangements in various settings, and on incentives and technical assistance required by employers to implement alternative working arrangements.

The Need for Action by Government and Unions

Although it is in the interest of society to encourage the spread of voluntary part-time work, a number of obstacles are created by laws and by union policies.

The Social Security and unemployment insurance laws discriminate against part-time workers by making them more expensive than full-time workers to the employer. Under the Social Security payroll tax, the employer contributes 6.65 percent of an employee's first $29,700 of wages. Two $20,000-a-year job-sharing employees cost $1,975 each, or $3,950 together. One full-time employee at $40,000 costs only $2,660. Similarly, under the present employer rate structure for unemployment compensation, hiring two part-time employees at $6,000 each would cost the employer $60 more per employee than hiring one full-time employee at $12,000.

recommendation 35

Tax-cost obstacles to part-time employment should be removed by computing the employer's contribution on the basis of how many full-time job equivalents are on the payroll, rather than how many actual employees the employer has.

A precedent is found in the recent decision of the federal government to change personnel accounting formulas so that the number of employees in a work unit is reckoned, not in terms of the absolute number of individuals, but in the number of full-time equivalents. (This change has been made to reduce the reluctance of managers to hire part-time workers).

The Social Security law discriminates also by penalizing older part-time workers. Individuals aged 65 to 72 suffer a reduction of benefits of $100 for every $200 they earn in excess of $5,500 a year.

recommendation 36

Congress should remove or significantly reduce the penalty against Social Security annuitants earning in excess of the exempt amount.

Many state unemployment insurance laws consider part-time employees ineligible for benefits because they are, in principle, not available for work, i.e., they cannot accept work at any time, without regard to days of the week or hours of the day.

recommendation 37

State unemployment laws should be amended to make the availability-for-work requirement for part-timers apply to work which is "suitable" in light of individual circumstances.

Unions view part-time work as a device that enables government to avoid its commitment to full employment, equal employment opportunity, equal pay, child care, and income security.

Statements of national labor union officials have often opposed the spread of permanent part-time employment and have deterred companies from using part-time staff. In fact, a smaller proportion of part-timers than full-timers are union-represented. The main union objections are these:

1. Expansion of part-time jobs is contrary to the interests of people who need full-time earnings. It will increase job competition and make unemployment worse. Converting full-time jobs into part-time jobs merely spreads unemployment; it does not create the needed new employment. Making more part-time jobs available will simply draw in people who are not now in the labor force, thus increasing the competition for jobs. Part-time employment may be acceptable to overcome labor shortages, but today's problem is labor surpluses.

2. Shorter workweeks or workyears for *all* employees, *without* loss of pay, is a priority union goal (as permitted by productivity gains). A focus on part-time employment may detract from this goal.

3. Since exploitation of part-timers is common and easy, labor standards are eroded. Part-timers are often denied fringe benefits, job security, and promotion opportunities. If part-time staffing were to increase, so would this inequitable treatment.

4. Part-time employment downgrades occupational status, institutionalizes the confinement of women to inferior work roles, and helps mainly those who need help the least.

5. People who would prefer part-time work are likely to be hard to organize and not good union members, because their main interests lie outside the workplace.

Some unions do recognize advantages in part-time employment. Local unions have bargained for part-time staffing, and include part-timers among their membership, for the following reasons:

1. Many people—people now outside the labor force as well as those currently fully employed—want working hours that are less than full time. Unions can serve them by winning part-time employment as an option.

2. In times of economic downturn, voluntary cutbacks in working time by some full-time workers to what amounts to part-time hours may be preferable to layoffs. More people with less work may be better than fewer people with more work. Both work sharing and job sharing—special versions of part-time employment—can accomplish this. If some workers prefer to stay permanently on a part-time schedule, so much the better; new jobs are created.

3. Some jobs appear to be part time by nature. Workers in these jobs

can be organized, and their work-life conditions improved, thus adding to union strength.

recommendation 38

Unions should seize the opportunity to gain new members by advocating the cause of the millions of workers who, for reasons of their own, either prefer permanent part-time status or choose it as a necessary step toward full-time status. (A case in point is the Selby, Minnesota, plant of Control Data Corporation, which has enabled welfare mothers to earn a living without giving up the care of their children.) *The legitimate interests of part-time workers include an end to wage discrimination, access to better-paying part-time jobs, and more equitable fringe benefits.*

Patsy Fryman, assistant to the president of the Communications Workers of America, has said, "The question is not whether to change work patterns; rather, the question is what kinds of changes are going to be accomplished, and how, and by whom. Said another way, new ways to work are going to happen and, in my opinion, it is a question of whether organized labor takes the lead in that change or whether it gets thrust upon us by other forces and we resist the change, therefore having less of an opportunity to impact on the changes made."[13]

As the number of women unionists grows, labor unions will become increasingly concerned with issues that are important to women workers. Day care and more flexible work scheduling are moving on to the negotiation agendas of a number of unions.

recommendation 39

Unions should poll their memberships periodically on issues like part-time employment, reduced workweeks, flexitime, the four-day week, and compensated work sharing as an alternative to layoffs, in order to stay abreast of evolving attitudes and needs.

Many collective bargaining contracts discriminate against part-time employees with respect to layoffs and recalls, placing them in the same category as probationary and temporary workers.

recommendation 40

Part-time workers should be subject to layoff and recall on the same basis as regular full-time employees, that is, according to seniority.

NOTES

1. Bureau of Labor Statistics, *Layoff, Recall, and Work-Sharing*

Schedules, Bulletin No. 1425-13 (Washington, D.C.: U.S. Government Printing Office, 1972).

2. Fred Best and James Mattesich, "Short-Time Compensation Systems in California and Europe," *Monthly Labor Review*, July 1980, pp. 13-22.

3. Ibid.

4. "Excerpts from Report by Legislative Analyst of California on State's Shared Work Unemployment Compensation Program," *Daily Labor Report*, April 14, 1981.

5. Best and Mattesich, "Short-Time Compensation Systems," *Monthly Labor Review,* July 1980.

6. Fred Best/National Commission for Employment Policy, *Exchanging Earnings for Leisure: Findings of An Exploratory National Survey on Work-Time Preferences* (Washington, D.C.: U.S. Department of Labor, Employment and Training Administration, 1980).

7. Louis Harris and Associates, Inc. *1979 Study of American Attitudes toward Pensions and Retirement* (New York: Johnson and Higgins, 1979).

8. Stephen R. McConnell, Dorothy Fleisher, Carolyn E. Usher, and Barbara Hade Kaplan, *Alternative Work Options for Older Workers: A Feasibility Study*, Executive Summary (Los Angeles: Andrus Gerontology Center, 1980).

9. Ibid.

10. Testimony of Dan McCorquodale before the California Senate Select Committee on Investment Priorities and Objectives. November 1, 1977.

11. "When Workers Say Never on Sunday," *Washington Post*, May 25, 1980.

12. Janice Neipert Hedges and Daniel E. Taylor, "Recent Trends in Worktime: Hours Edge Downward," *Monthly Labor Review*, March 1980, pp. 3-11.

13. Patsy Fryman, "A Labor View on Alternative Work Patterns," remarks at a conference on "The Focus on Alternative Work Patterns," Seattle, summer of 1979.

7.

Work Schedules and Family Time

Profound changes are taking place in family structure, in labor-force patterns, in workers' values, and in workers' expectations about their jobs. The "linear" life plan is breaking down. These changes in workers' family and personal lives have outstripped the ability of the workplace to accommodate them. Mounting stress and a decline in the quality of life are consequences of the dissonance. Not surprisingly, the 1980 White House Conference on Families adopted as its top recommendation "A call for family-oriented personnel policies—flexitime, leave policies, shared and part-time jobs, transfer policies."[1]

In the University of Michigan's *1977 Quality of Employment Survey*, a large representative sample of American workers was asked, "How much do your job and family life interfere with each other?" Over 10 percent of both men and women answered "a lot." An additional 25 percent or more answered "somewhat."

Those who answered either "a lot" or "somewhat" were asked a further question, "In what ways do they interfere with each other?" The largest single source of interference was work time, with 39 percent of the group responding, "Excessive amount of work prevents worker from spending enough time with family." Another 5 percent said, "Worker wants time spent at work to be spent with family." Another 2.7 percent said, "Vacation schedule is inconvenient," or "Worker does not get enough vacation."

The full sample of workers was next asked, "Would you like to spend less time working so that you could spend more time with your spouse and children, even if it meant having less money, or would you like to spend more time working in order to have more money, even if it meant spending less time with your spouse and children?" Forty percent of both men and women said they would prefer less time working and more time with the family, even if it meant less pay. Only 12 percent of men and 5 percent of women voted for more time working and less time with the family.[2]

A major source of interference between work and family is the fact that many institutions on which families depend operate on their own fixed hours: Schools start at 9:00 a.m. and end at 3:00 p.m.; City Hall opens at 9:00 a.m. and closes at 5:00 p.m.; and the doctor is in the office from 10:00 a.m. to 2:00 p.m. (At least the supermarket is open until midnight!) The workplace itself is often one of the institutions with fixed and inconvenient hours, and workers and their families are the ones who have to adjust and adapt. The key difficulty is meshing all the home and family-life schedules with the workplace schedule.

Several current developments make time management problems for workers particularly severe:

☐ The American family of the 1980s has changed markedly. The "traditional" family we knew in the 1950s—the classic nuclear group of Dick-and-Jane fame (husband-breadwinner and wife-homemaker, who stays home with two children)—has dwindled to a small statistical minority. Only 13 percent of all families fit that definition. In 1978, labor-force participation rates of women in all marital categories ranged from 47.6 percent among married women living with their husbands to 74 percent among divorced women (see figure 4). Today, among married women with school-age children, close to 59 percent are employed outside the home. We have dual-earner families, single-parent families, extended families.

☐ Time problems are intractable for many traditional families; they are more so for dual-earner and single-parent families. Single-parent families have only one instead of two pairs of hands to do home and child-care chores. Most dual earners and single parents work because they have to (or believe they have to). Even if they work because they want to, the problems are no less real.

☐ Pluralism in family structure is increasing. Life-styles are even more diverse than family structures (see figure 5). Each worker's needs for personal time and family time change in the course of his or her life cycle. Since family systems are no longer stable, a worker's time needs can change quickly.

☐ Many people in the labor force today have primary responsibility for someone else at home—a child, an aged relative, a retired spouse. Their number will grow. At the same time, success in most professional, managerial, and sales jobs demands a near-total commitment to the job, often in excess of full-time hours. The effort to achieve success both in one's career and in a primary parenting (or dependent-caretaking) role often stretches people to the breaking point. There is not enough time to do both well, and social institutions are arrayed against it.

□ The linear life plan is increasingly in question. More and more people find it hard to make sense of going to school until age 17 or 21, then working full time for 40 or 50 years, and then abruptly retiring to a life of leisure. Already many are trying to order their lives differently, but they are doing so in the face of institutional practices that discourage it. As people's interests and their uses for nonworking time change, work schedules will have to change. The mixing of education with work, work with leisure, and work outside the home with work inside the home cannot be reconciled with traditional patterns.

□ As workers' expectations about their jobs rise, they want good jobs, higher wages, and challenges. But lots of jobs are dull jobs. Often technological advance is carelessly allowed to take the interest, not just the drudgery, out of jobs. Dull, unfulfilled work life spills over into home life and personal time.

Figure 4
Labor Force Participation Rates of Women,
by Marital Status: 1970 and 1978

Percent in civilian labor force

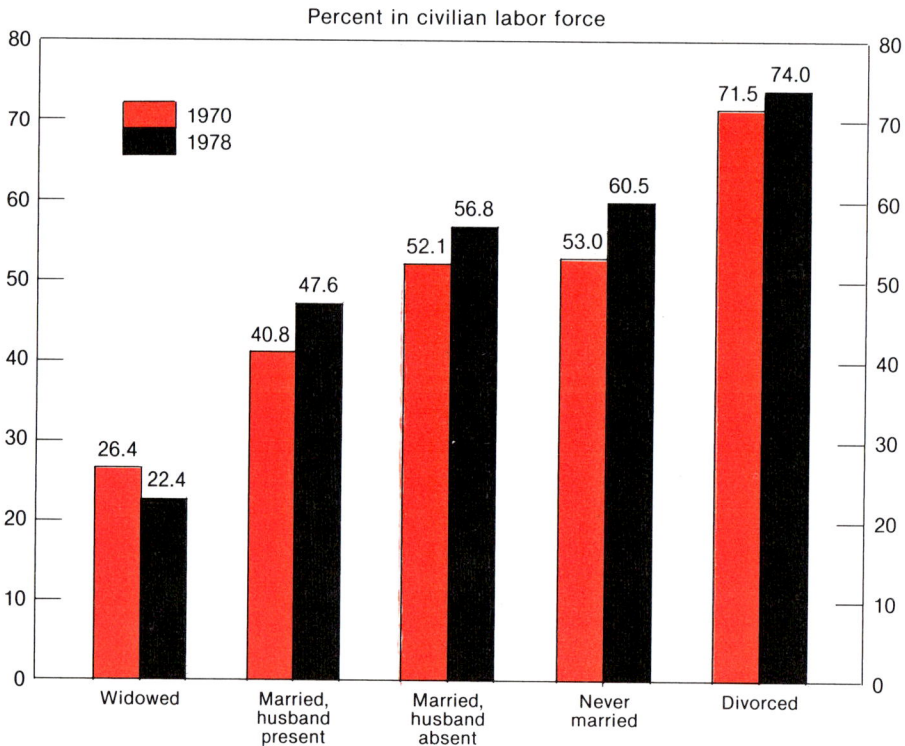

Source: U.S. Bureau of Labor Statistics.

☐   The values shaping workers' lives are changing in fundamental ways: (1) leisure time has become more important, and workers prefer to take it in longer blocks; (2) personal development has become more important, not only on the job but in social and cultural pursuits; (3) quality of life, both at the workplace and away from work, has become more important; (4) roles and behaviors traditionally assigned to the sexes are being challenged and altered by men as well as women; (5) what used to be workers' privileges have become expectations, and then demands, with workers asking for a fair share of control over work life.

☐   Although values are always changing, the changes now occurring are at the heart of the worker-workplace relationship. The traditional role of the employer is being challenged because the workplace has so long resisted change. The workplace, as well as the worker, must adapt. Work life and home life increasingly are interdependent.

Figure 5
Types of Households, 1960, 1975, 1990

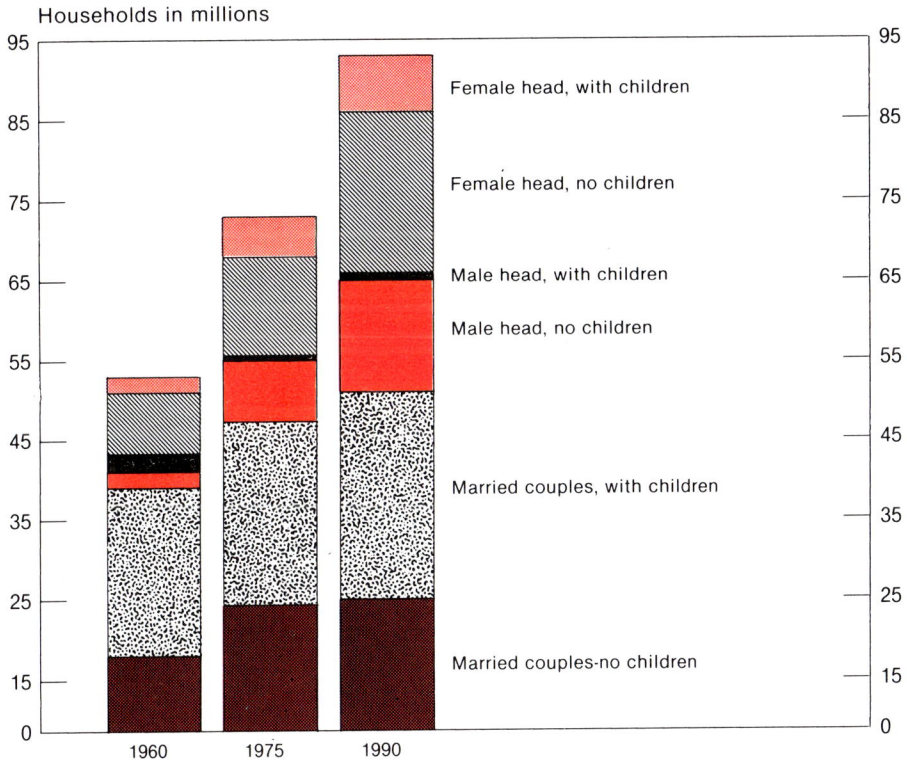

Source: U.S. Bureau of Labor Statistics.

Despite the compelling evidence of conflict between work life and home life deduced from national survey data and observations of social trends, few employers see family and personal-time management as a problem to their workers. It is certainly not a priority item in the boardrooms of American corporations. The business press gives it little attention. How can there be such a gulf between society's views and employers' views of the same facts?

Conflict between work life and home life is not discussed at work. Women are more directly affected by it than men, but no career-oriented woman employee dares to reveal family problems or to let work-family conflicts intrude. Men, if they feel the problem personally, are not likely to let it color others' perceptions of their masculinity or devotion to the work ethic. As one chief executive officer remarked cynically, "Most CEOs don't care about their own families. Why should they care about the problems employees have with their families?"

If workers are to be regarded as assets, as so many corporate annual reports say they are, employers need to take a long range, productivity-based view of them. Personal events in workers' lives affect their workplace performance, and vice versa. Control Data Corporation's famous Employee Advisory Resource program incorporates this view, which recognizes that workers' needs for time at home, time at work, and time at school vary, not only with the person, but within the person, over his or her life cycle. The policy holds that the employer should act to improve the interaction between work life and home life as long as it is in the organization's long-run economic interest to do so.

Can and Should Companies Do Something about Family Life and Time Management?

The trends that give rise to workers' problems of meshing personal time, family time, and work time are social trends. Does an employer have the capability, acting alone, to cope with such broad changes? Can new work schedules like flexitime and job sharing really have a noticeable impact? After all, work schedules are only one small variable amid a host of institutional and personal constants; can they make a difference to a worker's family life and personal-time needs?

Even if employers can do something about the problem, should they? To what extent should they get mixed up in the private lives of their employees? In order to know what to do, an employer would have to gather information about employees' home lives and personal time. And employer action, even when intended for the worker's benefit, might mean employer presence, if not interference, in private lives. Both legality and ethics are at issue. Does action on behalf of workers' family lives and personal-time needs push an employer into paternalism, or into the social-responsibility business, contrary to free-market principles? Will employers, by default, have to provide social services that other institutions (schools, churches, families, governments) have abandoned?

And there is another concern. Work-schedule flexibility could, in the present social climate, have adverse side-effects among traditional families in which roles are still sex-assigned. Women in such families might end up doing more homework and child care, rather than less, and therefore undergoing more, rather than less, imbalance and stress.

In the face of these reservations, what should employers do about workers' problems of family life and time management?

In dealing with the problem of conflict and tensions between work life and home life, employers should try to follow a course of action that is facilitating rather than restrictive. Their policies should be designed to increase workers' options and self-management and, at the same time, to enlarge the potential for improved worker performance on the job.

recommendation 41

The employer's objective can be simply to remove barriers and relax rules, rather than to add incentives and supports. Instead of taking responsibility for solving workers' problems, the employer can enable workers to solve their own. Several new work schedules, especially flexitime, flexiplace, and job sharing, are of this nature. For example, flexitime permits workers to set their own schedules, but it also permits them *not* to do so. It does not require anyone to alter his or her life-style. Similarly, cafeteria benefits permit workers to choose what best suits their needs, rather than to take or leave a set program; and some employers offer to broker between employee child-care needs and the services available in the community, instead of providing an on-site, employer-paid day-care center. Another action employers can take is to include education about work and family issues as part of supervisory and management training programs.

Faced with diversity, change, and unpredictability in life-styles and family structures, the employer's best approach is to be adaptable and not to mount specific programs for specific needs without first consulting employees. Most new work schedules increase the number of options workers have and their control over their life patterns. They require very small direct outlays by the employer and have potential for productivity improvement.

recommendation
42

Employer policies regarding workers' family life and personal time management problems should be applicable to employees regardless of age, status, and sex, rather than directed only toward women.

Older workers, students, and the working poor, among others, need as much help from business policies on work-life/home-life conflicts as do women with young children. In the future, working male parents will need the same opportunities to balance work life with home life. To conceive employer policies in terms of the special needs of married women without consideration of the needs of single people and married men, is to restrict and weaken them unnecessarily. The fact that some new work schedules, such as flexitime and job sharing, now benefit women employees with young children more than they benefit other groups is a passing thing, the result of current cultural conditions.

How Can New Work Patterns Help?

The state of knowledge as to how new work schedules actually assist workers in their time-management problems leaves much to be desired. This in itself is evidence of how little attention has been paid to the question. Of course, flexitime, to take one example, cannot lengthen the day beyond 24 hours, nor shorten the workweek of 40 hours. But flexitime can let workers organize their days more efficiently and create more usable time for themselves, even though they work no less.

Part-time employment and job sharing permit workers to devote some (rather than all or none) of their working time to paid employment, but at the price of lower earnings.

Based on case-study research, some tentative conclusions about the effects of flexitime on workers' family life and personal time can be offered:

☐ When the more flexible varieties of flexitime are adopted, workers gain time for family life and personal activities, and they make better use of that time. They get up earlier in the day, sleep less, and use less time to commute to and from work. But if a flexitime schedule is not very flexible, such time gains don't materialize.

☐ External conditions also influence the outcome. If workers are unable to take advantage of being on flexitime because car pools, spouses, or institutions (such as schools or government offices) have conflicting schedules, they gain neither flexibility nor additional time for family life and personal needs.

☐ Flexitime helps some, but not all, employees to manage family stress, depending on the magnitude of the problem. If the stress is deeply rooted, the contribution of flexitime may be irrelevant.

☐   Except in the least traditional families, flexitime makes little difference as to who does what at home. Husbands and wives do the same tasks with flexitime as without.

Because so little knowledge has been established regarding the interaction of work and family, employers should take an experimental approach to new work schedules insofar as they are intended to improve the family life and personal time management problems of workers.

recommendation **43**

Employers should try to accommodate the diversity of their employees' family-time and personal-time needs by offering several new work schedules rather than just one. These may include flexitime, flexiplace, combinations of flexitime with job sharing and career part-time jobs, and compressed work-weeks.

recommendation **44**

1.   Flexitime and flexiplace permit workers the greatest ease of meshing full-time work and family schedules.

Maximum flexibility in the distribution of work hours, consistent with job requirements, gives employees the greatest chance to improve job performance. A variable-day version of flexitime with minimum core hours should therefore be adopted where possible. (By contrast, a mere one-hour "window" for start-work and quit-work times will not help parents cope with child care before and after school.) The more employers who offer flexitime, the better. That way, both parents have work-schedule options, and the potential for solving schedule conflicts is doubled.

Insofar as work-home schedule conflicts arise because of geography—the distance of the office from home and school—flexiplace can help. When job requirements permit, let the work site be located where workers' home and family needs are located.

2.   Job sharing, career part-time employment, and flexiplace reduce the amount of time required for work and commuting, and thus let workers gain time for family needs.

Flexiplace, by cutting commuting time, can reclaim several hours a week for workers. (If some of the commuting time was used productively, as in reading on the bus, the net gain would be less.) Flexitime may also reduce commuting time because it permits employees to commute during off-peak hours.

Job sharing and other forms of part-time employment let workers trade less work and less income for more time. Many full-time workers make this trade-off when it is available; many others cannot stand the loss of earnings or career status.

recommendation 45

We recommend that employers experiment with various levels of part-time work, especially three-quarters time and four-fifths time, to test the attractiveness of various earnings and career prospects. Reducing the workweek as little as 20 percent can increase discretionary time by 50 to 80 percent!

3. The compressed workweek sometimes eases and sometimes complicates work-home conflicts. However, it can be of great benefit in relieving the strains of shift work.

Parents responsible for young children often find the 10- to 12-hour day destructive of home life, although the three-day weekend compensates somewhat. The addition of flexible hours helps, but the degree of flexibility workers actually have is limited by the length of the day. (A ten-hour day, beginning after the children go to school, destroys the evening.) Some employers who have compressed workweeks (for example, Physio-Control) avoid flexibility in hours for precisely this reason. However, other employers (for example, the Board of Governors of the Federal Reserve System) do have flexitime in combination with a compressed workweek. The work pattern used successfully here is the 5/4-9 version of compressed workweeks, which has nine-hour rather than ten-hour days. Perhaps the best option of all is maxiflex—flexitime without core hours on all days, and with debit and credit hours possibilities—which permits workers who prefer to compress 40 hours a week into four days to do so.

recommendation 46

We recommend that employers consider compressed workweeks to ease the personal and family dislocations caused by shift work and involuntary overtime. Workers in continuous-process industries with rotating shifts have found three 12-hour shifts a great help in relieving the physiological and psychological

upsets and the loss of personal time that go with five eight-hour shifts. Managers find that it reduces coverage problems, turnover, and shoddy work. Many chemical plants and oil refineries in Canada and the United States as well as in Europe are moving to this schedule. (Shell Canada has such a schedule, described more fully in the casebook for this policy study, *New Work Schedules in Practice*.)

In order to understand their employees' work-time/family-time problems, employers should conduct regular surveys on that subject, with the cooperation of the union, where there is one.

recommendation 47

Already some companies conduct sophisticated surveys of employee attitudes. Control Data Corporation does so regularly and, as a result, was able to anticipate an impending problem with performance appraisals and take preventative action. These surveys can be more widely and systematically used to gain information about personal time and the management of family-life problems that employees are experiencing.

As another means of obtaining information about workers' work and family problems, employers should make use of family-impact studies.

recommendation 48

Some of an employer's personnel (as well as production) policies may have unintended adverse effects on workers' family life and personal time. A family-impact statement, akin to an environmental-impact statement, would assess what happens to the meshing of workers' schedules because of the employer's time demands. For example, the extraordinary amount of time some workers spend commuting—two and one-half hours a day in a recent study in Washington, D.C.—may be due partly to employers' fixed work hours. Companies with rotating shift-work schedules are finding out how those schedules affect workers and their ability to operate the plant.

NOTES

1. The White House Conference on Families, *Listening to America's Families: Action for the 80's* (Washington, D.C.: U.S. Government Printing Office, 1980).
2. Robert P. Quinn and Graham L. Staines, *The 1977 Quality of Employment Survey* (Ann Arbor, Mich.: University of Michigan, Institute for Social Research, 1979).

8.

Work Schedules and Personal Time

The social revolution of the 1960s and 1970s sharpened the awareness of many people that the claims of work, family, and personal needs were out of balance; work received excessive attention from men, while families received excessive attention from women. People of all ages, most of all the young, resolved to find a better equilibrium.

As a result of these corrective efforts, a myth has grown up that we now live in an age of leisure. The reality is that most people still work as long and as hard as ever. Many women, in fact, are working for pay, as well as working in their homes. Some men have begun to share home duties. Work schedules, by and large, pay little heed to the desire for a new equilibrium. The West Europeans, with their tradition of frequent religious holidays, have (except in Britain) gone much further than the United States toward shortening the workyear, but they are still behind us with respect to the workday and workweek.

The difficulty of balancing work, family, and personal needs for people who work five eight-hour days a week stands out clearly in table 9. In the case of dual-earner families, at least 40 to 50 hours a week are lost due to the second earner's work and commuting times. For single parents, the difficulty is even greater. Since the day has only 16 waking hours, any time put into one pocket of life must be drawn from another.

We speak of "personal needs" rather than "leisure" because the latter is too narrow. It omits education and other forms of self-improvement, the importance of which will grow as the pace of economic and social change speeds up.

In the case of people who need full-time earnings, the most obvious way to gain more personal time is to reduce the workweek without re-

Table 9
Effects of Flexitime on Family Life and Personal Activity

Item	Score[a]
With standard fixed hours, the most difficult things to do are:	
Spend afternoon time with my child.	5.9
Have breakfast time with my child.	5.3
Pursue educational opportunities (formal and informal).	5.2
Shopping and household chores.	5.1
Engage in recreational pursuits and hobbies.	4.9
Spend time with my spouse or partner during the week.	4.9
Pick up my child after school or from child care.	4.7
Have relaxed evenings during the week.	4.7
See friends during the week.	4.5
Commute to and from work.	4.5
With standard fixed hours, the least difficult things to do are:	
Share lunchtime or coffee break with friends at work.	3.4
Have dinner with my spouse or partner and child during the week.	3.7

	Change in Score[b]
The biggest positive effects of flexitime are that it is easier to:	
Spend afternoon time with my child.	2.3
Spend time in the evening with my child.	1.8
See friends during the workweek.	1.7
Engage in recreational pursuits and hobbies.	1.7
Pursue educational opportunities (formal and informal).	1.6
Do shopping and household chores.	1.6
Spend time with my spouse or partner during the week.	1.5
Have relaxed evenings during the workweek.	1.3
Have dinner with my spouse or partner and child during the week.	1.0
Commute to and from work.	.9
The negative effects of flexitime are that it is harder to:[c]	
Have breakfast time with my child.	- .3
Share lunchtime or coffee break with friends at work.	- .2

Notes:

[a]Average of 34 employees in two agencies on a scale where 7 was "very difficult" and 1 was "very easy"; midpoint=4. Both pre- and post-flexitime surveys were taken during the school year.

[b]These changes are statistically significant compared to fixed work hours and a comparison group.

[c]Not statistically significant.

Source: Richard A. Winett, Michael S. Neale, and Kenneth R. Williams, "The Effects of Flexible Work Schedule on Urban Family with Young Children: Quasi-Experimental, Ecological Studies," unpublished paper (Blacksburg, Va.: Virginia Polytechnic Institute and State University, 1979).

ducing weekly pay. The labor movement in the United States has been struggling for years to do just that.

People frequently voice the objection that such a reduction will also reduce productivity. This reflects a misunderstanding: there is no rigid relationship between the length of the workweek and productivity. Productivity may rise, fall, or stand still while hours per week decline. The true reason people raise this issue is their concern that if productivity does not rise in proportion to the decrease of hours per week, unit costs will increase. On the other hand, shortening the workweek may reinvigorate workers, sharpen their wits, and thus enable them to increase output per hour (or any other definition of productivity) enough to offset the reduction of hours.

Although the eight-hour day and 40-hour week still prevail, inroads are steadily being made into the 2,080-hour year. However, they are being made piecemeal, through additional holidays, personal days off, and longer vacations (and through unpaid absenteeism and partly paid sick leave). These "days off" are undoubtedly reflected in the International Labour Organisation's recent report that the average U.S. workweek is 35.6 hours, the shortest of all among Western industrialized nations.[1]

In certain industries, unions have managed to shorten the workyear significantly. For example, the automotive industry's 1979 contract with the United Auto Workers provides 26 paid personal holidays, which employees *must* take and for which they cannot accept pay in lieu of time off. This program has two purposes: to lessen the rigors of the automotive assembly line and to create jobs for younger workers. When paid vacation, statutory holidays, paid personal holidays, and personal-absence days off are all counted in, an auto worker entitled to three-weeks vacation with pay will receive 126 paid days off over a three-year period—an average of 42 days off with pay per year. Another ten days a year would bring it to 52 per year, equivalent to a 32-hour week.[2]

A large proportion of paid days off are service-connected. That is, the longer the service an employee has had with a given employer, the more vacation and sick leave the employee earns. In addition, managements tend to be more lenient in granting extensions of time off to long-service than to new employees.

According to Congress's Joint Economic Committee report of November 1980, "The average vacation period in the U.S. is still only two weeks, reflecting the relatively short average job tenure in private industry. But with many establishments offering four to six weeks of vacation to experienced workers, vacation patterns may change significantly as the new entrants of the last two decades gain seniority on the job. Length of job tenure with a particular company is the usual basis for vacation eligibility in the

U.S. In 1978 it was estimated that average job tenure was 3.6 years, down from 3.9 years in 1973. This reduction was the result of the large labor-force influx of teen-agers and women. In 1978 as many as 28 percent of the employed population had been on their jobs less than one year, and the average length of vacation was 2.0 weeks."[3]

In other words, had there not been so many new entrants into the work force in the 1970s, it would be easier to see that the length of the workyear for long-service workers has substantially declined. Many new entrants are just as responsible for raising families as are long-service employees, and undoubtedly have as much need for personal time, but they cannot get it.

Personal Time for Education

The need for further education, not necessarily in traditional four-year colleges, will be greater than ever before. Not only people entering the work force for the first time, or reentering it, but also those already in will have need for such education. Employers and their employees will have to cooperate in shaping work schedules that satisfy the needs of the organization and, at the same time, enable employees to take advantage of the opportunities available.

The Joint Economic Committee report of November 1980 points out that, although small, private four-year colleges are having a rough time, "many of the public community colleges are flourishing as they attract older individuals returning to formal education—often while continuing to work. The median age of community college students is 27 years, compared to nearly 21 for the traditional four-year college. About 49 percent of full-time and 87 percent of part-time community college students are employed in either a full-time or substantial part-time capacity (including mothers with children at home)."[4]

Several cases on the West Coast bring home this connection between new work schedules and time for education. For example, production workers at Sercel Industries, a manufacturer of instruments in Redmond, Washington, work semicontinuous shifts in a compressed week with flexible hours. The average age of the employees is 21, and their educational level is low: the majority are women, including many high school dropouts. Since the new work schedule was instituted, many of the employees have begun taking classes at the local community college on their own time.

Physio-Control Corporation, also in Redmond, Washington, manufactures electronic medical instruments. The company operates three different work schedules for its production workers: two compressed workweek schedules running from Monday through Thursday, and shift work of three 12-hour days on Friday, Saturday, and Sunday. This is a high-skill, fast-growing organization, which depends on outside institutions to provide education and technical training and offers 100 percent reimbursement of tuition. Of its 788 employees in 1980, 158 received tuition aid; 85 percent of the weekend shift workers were attending school, mainly to finish four years of college.

At Group Health Cooperative of Puget Sound in Seattle, Washington, 135 employees in the accounting and billing department went on to flexitime schedules in 1979. Soon afterward, some of the clerical employees with less than average schooling began taking college courses before or after core hours in their schedule.

Two government agencies in Washington, D.C., which introduced flexitime in 1978, found that flexitime had made the pursuit of educational opportunities substantially easier for employees. In addition, flexitime facilitated shopping and household chores and created more time for recreation and association with friends during the week.

Increasing the Availability of Personal Time

The number of ways in which the work schedule can be adjusted to make personal time available when it is needed, in blocks of needed length and without impairing the enterprise, is legion. With flexitime, for example, employees can work a five-day 40-hour week and yet make adjustments from day to day to suit their needs. The compressed workweek allows employees to work a 40-hour week but have three-day weekends.

On the other hand, a worker who wanted to take educational courses every day for a substantial part of the day might arrange a part-time job or a job-sharing arrangement. Part-time employment and job sharing can also enable employees to work full days, but fewer than five days a week, thus freeing two or three additional days a week for personal use. If an employee needs a much larger block of time—for a three-month full-time college course or a long family vacation, for example—he or she might work regular 40-hour weeks most of the year and then take the necessary long period either as paid vacation or as a combination of paid and unpaid leave. Still another possibility is the sabbatical, whereby the employee takes as long as six months or a year off from work every seventh year.

Every employee has to make a trade-off between earnings and personal time, but the range of options is usually so narrow that employees' true preferences remain unclear. How much income would employees be willing to trade for how much personal time? Does the answer depend on the form in which personal time is offered?

The National Commission for Employment Policy, hoping to get a handle on these questions, sponsored a nationwide survey by Louis Harris and Associates in August 1978. The survey put several questions to a representative sample of American workers. One asked the interviewees to choose between a 2 percent pay raise and the following alternative ways of receiving equivalent time off: 10 minutes off each workday, 50 minutes off one workday each week, five additional days of paid annual vacation per year, earlier retirement by seven workdays a year. Sixty-four percent of the sample said they would prefer one or the other of the time-off alternatives; only 36 percent said they would prefer the pay raise. Very few chose the ten minutes off each workday, but 17 percent chose the 50 minutes off one workday each week, 26 percent chose the five additional days of paid annual vacation, and 19 percent chose the earlier retirement.

The next question asked, in effect, "If you were offered a 10 percent pay raise, what portion of that raise would you be willing to trade for equivalent amounts of free time in various forms?" Once again, the forms included a shortened workday, a shortened workweek, added vacation, sabbaticals, and earlier retirement. The percentage of workers willing to trade all or part of the 10 percent pay raise varied substantially as between one form of free time and another. Only 26 percent of the workers, for example, were prepared to exchange all or part of their 10 percent raise for a reduced workday. However, 44 percent were willing to trade for a reduced workweek; 51 percent were willing to trade for earlier retirement; 65 percent were willing to trade for longer sabbatical leaves; and 66 percent were willing to trade for longer vacations.

A third question brought the interviewees back to their own schedules. "What is the largest portion of your *current* yearly income that you would be willing to give up for various forms of free time?" The interviewees were offered 11 degrees of sacrifice of current earnings, ranging from 0 to 50 percent. Each of these options was matched with an equivalent amount of free time in the form of shorter workdays, shorter workweeks, added vacations, sabbatical leave, or earlier retirement. The answers, although less enthusiastic than those for the 10 percent pay raise, followed a similar pattern: 23 percent of the sample were willing to exchange part of current earnings for a shorter workday; 26 percent were willing to exchange for a reduced workweek; 36 percent were willing to exchange for earlier retirement; 42 percent were willing to exchange some current income for additional vacation; and the same percentage opted for sabbatical leave.[5]

If the Harris findings are anywhere near the mark, they indicate that 30 to 40 million American workers are prepared to trade part of their current earnings for equivalent amounts of free time, particularly if the free time is in longer blocks, such as added vacation or sabbatical leave.

The Harris findings have been partially confirmed by the experience of California's Santa Clara County government.

Santa Clara County

In the spring of 1976 Santa Clara County, anticipating a deficit for the next fiscal year, proposed to its local unions of the Service Employees International Union that all employees should accept a reduction of 6.25

percent in both work hours and pay. This would have reduced work hours from 80 for each two-week period to 75 hours. The unions countered with a proposal for voluntary work sharing, which the county accepted, with the option of taking more drastic measures if the voluntary plan failed. The plan went into effect even though the deficit did not materialize.

Under the agreement, each employee may request a reduction of work time and pay of either 2.5, 5, 10, or 20 percent for six months at a time. The time reduction may be taken in the form of fewer hours per day, fewer days per week, or longer blocks of time away from work. Employee and supervisor must agree on the arrangements. The arrangements must not produce compulsory overtime for other employees, or speed-ups for those who choose to reduce their work time, or for others. However, some temporary hiring is permitted and has, in fact, occurred, which somewhat reduces the savings. Fringe benefits are not affected by reductions, except for retirement contributions, which are tied to earnings.

The number of volunteers for work reduction has ranged from 15 percent of the work force at the beginning (October 1976) to 4.5 percent in October 1979. The average amount of time and pay reduction per volunteer has been about 10 percent. The number of volunteers depends on their expectations of possible layoffs and on the impact of inflation and recession. It is notable, however, that while the number of volunteers for reduced working hours declined between 1976 and 1979, the volume of part-time work and job sharing, which are also encouraged by the contract, steadily rose.

The contract between the county and the unions also provides a wide range of training opportunities for workers. These opportunities are extensively taken, and the tuition-aid fund is always fully used. A disproportionately high number of clerical and blue-collar employees avail themselves of the tuition aid.

Another interesting case of trading money for personal time is that of Harman Mirrors in Bolivar, Tennessee. Many production workers there, in a quality-of-working-life program, improved quality and speed of output to the extent that they were able to finish eight hours' work in six. When management offered them a choice between a two-hour reduction of the workday and a proportionate increase of daily earnings, the workers, through their UAW local, chose the two hours. Some used the freed time to work on their home farms, but others used it to take part in a wide variety of educational programs arranged at the workplace.

A historical precedent for the Bolivar tradeoff is found in the old British system of "job and finish," under which workers are assigned a day's work with the understanding that they are free to leave the workplace as soon as the job is done.

Further confirmation of the Harris survey appears in the record of federal and state employees who volunteered to change from full-time to part-time jobs (see pp. 99-100 of this report).

NOTES

1. Survey by the International Labour Organisation, reported in the *Wall Street Journal,* February 20, 1981.

2. Irving Bluestone, "Bluestone Sees Pension Increases as 'Highest Priority' of GM Contract," *World of Work Report,* December 1979.

3. Joint Economic Committee, *Human Resources and Demographics: Characteristics of People and Policy,* Special Study on Economic Change (Washington, D.C.: Joint Economic Committee of Congress, 1980).

4. Ibid.

5. Fred Best/National Commission for Employment Policy, *Exchanging Earnings for Leisure: Findings of an Exploratory National Survey on Work-Time Preferences* (Washington, D.C.: Department of Labor, Employment and Training Administration, 1980).

9.

Union Concerns:
The Dangers
of Overtime Abuse

The usage of new work schedules is lower among labor union members than among unorganized employees. In only 7 percent of all flexitime companies in a 1977 survey did union members constitute as many as half of their flexitime employees. In a recent Bureau of Labor Statistics report, only 7.3 percent of all full-time nonfarm wage and salary workers who were members of unions (including employee associations) were on flexible schedules; among nonunion employees, the flexitime usage rate was nearly double that, 13.7 percent.[1]

Part of this gap in the usage of flexitime as between union and nonunion members is associated with occupational and industrial patterns of usage. For example, flexitime is much more common among sales workers, managers, and administrators than among craft workers, operatives, and laborers—occupations that are more highly unionized. Flexitime is also used at more than average rates in industries such as wholesale and retail trade, finance and insurance, other services, and public administration, where union membership is far smaller than in manufacturing.

Compressed workweeks also are used less frequently among labor union members than among nonunion employees. There was little or no union membership among compressed workweek employees in 84 percent of the companies in a 1977 survey (but in one user organization out of seven in this survey, half or more of the compressed workweek employees were union members).[2]

In the United States overall, 2.2 percent of union members were on compressed schedules in 1980, while 2.9 percent of nonunion members had compressed schedules. But in the case of compressed workweeks, it is not apparent that the usage rate gap between union and nonunion employees is related to either occupation or industry. For example, in 1980 the highest usage rates of compressed schedules occurred among service workers and operatives, public administration, miscellaneous services, and construction industries. The smallest usage rate for compressed schedules occurred among managers and administrators, clerical workers, and sales workers, and in the mining, finance, insurance, and real estate industries. There is no clear pattern of high or low union membership corresponding to the pattern of high and low compressed workweek usage in these industries and occupations.[3]

Many local unions and their members have been sufficiently attracted to flexitime and compressed workweeks to negotiate them with employers, but leaders at the international level (with exceptions, such as the UAW) have been either cautious or opposed. One of the main grounds of opposition has been the fear that employers might exploit these schedules to breach the established rules governing overtime.

1. Although most collective bargaining agreements impose premium pay after eight hours of work in a day, and federal law requires overtime pay after eight hours for workers on government contracts, all compressed weeks imply workdays in excess of eight hours. They call for nine, ten, or even twelve hours a day. If employers had to pay overtime rates for these extra hours per day, compressed workweeks would be uneconomic.

2. Flexitime with fixed workdays of eight hours or less raise no problems of overtime pay, and labor unions have gone along with them. But when a flexitime schedule permits workdays of variable length and the crediting and debiting of work hours, it offers great potential, not only for improving workers' quality of life, but for employer abuse of overtime. The danger is that managers may subtly pressure flexitime workers to stay late "voluntarily," so that company needs can be met without premium pay.

Four federal statutes govern. The Fair Labor Standards Act requires overtime pay after 40 hours in a week for employees in interstate commerce and public administration. The Walsh-Healy Public Contracts Act requires overtime pay after eight hours a day for employees working directly on federal government contracts of more than $10,000. The Contract Work Hours and Safety Standards Act requires overtime pay after eight hours on federal construction contracts covered by the Davis-Bacon Act. Finally, the Federal Pay Act, which applies to all nonexempt federal workers, requires overtime pay after eight hours a day or 40 hours a week. These laws exempt many supervisory and other white-collar employees, who have therefore enjoyed the greatest freedom to work out flexitime programs. Many blue-collar workers would like similar flexibility but feel hemmed in by the laws that protect them.

The national union leaders' abhorrence of proposals to tamper with the overtime laws has deep roots. It took many bloody battles to gain the eight-hour day and the 40-hour week, after a long period of exploitation and depression. During those years, overtime work at premium pay was a cherished reward for seniority.

As affluence spread, the economic need for overtime work diminished in some industries to the point where management found it impossible to induce employees to accept it. Today, even in a recession, workers are strongly conscious of conflicts among family, leisure, and work, and young people are determined to balance those three factors more satisfyingly than their parents did. International Harvester in 1980 lost a devastating strike when the UAW rejected a proposal for mandatory overtime. More and more, overtime is worked on a purely voluntary basis; premium pay may or may not offset the desire for personal time.

In the 1970s and 1980s a few local unions, taking heed of their members' changing priorities, began to test new work schedules, sometimes waiving premium pay in exchange for greater flexibility. The national unions have remained unyielding on principle, but have allowed the locals to experiment. This pattern applied also when the 94th Congress enacted the federal program of alternative work schedules.

Several local unions on the West Coast have found successful ways of instituting more favorable patterns of work without giving up the protection of the law.

☐ Local 21 of the International Federation of Professional and Technical Employees, at the request of its members, negotiated flexitime agreements with private and public employers in California. About 1,000 members, all white-collar workers, were covered. The local developed several guidelines for safety: (1) the contract must contain explicit language about workers' protection and provide an appropriate grievance procedure for overtime disputes; (2) the agreement must hold the *employees* accountable for meeting their time requirements; and (3) there must be cooperation and good faith between union and management. No unsolved problems have arisen.

The union's contract with Alameda County sets up an 80-hour pay period rather than a 40-hour week or eight-hour day. Employees may work as few or as many hours a day as they choose, provided that (1) they are present during core hours; (2) they don't start before 7:00 a.m. or quit after 6:00 p.m.; and (3) they remain on the job when necessary to get the job done. When an employee requests, and the supervisor permits, hours worked before 7:00 a.m. or after 6:00 p.m. are credited. Debits cannot be carried forward beyond the time period in which they are incurred. Overtime is defined as work which (1) is requested by the supervisor, (2) requires the employee to arrive before or stay beyond his or her normal hours, and (3) causes the employee to work more than 80 hours in the pay period.

☐ In the State of Washington, Local 8 of the Office and Professional Employees Union negotiated with the Group Health Cooperative of Puget

Sound for flexitime with debits and credits, covering 135 clerical and supervisory employees in a single department. Management resisted. Problems were resolved by a joint committee. Other departments are now considering a similar deal.

Under the agreement, each employee may work as few as three and a half or as many as eleven hours a day, as long as the total at the end of a week is 40. The existing contract, which calls for overtime after eight hours in a day, was waived.

To make the agreement work, the respective responsibilities for getting the work done were agreed on in writing between each employee and his or her supervisor. If employees want to alter their planned hours, they must arrange, with the help of the supervisor, for substitute coverage. Management has provided the cross-training to make this feasible.

Overtime in this plan is defined as hours in excess of 40 a week, which are approved by the supervisor. If a worker's hourly work sheet shows fewer than 40 hours of work, the unworked hours must be accounted for as sick leave, vacation, or leave without pay. If employees take sick leave or vacation time off, they are permitted to work only long enough to bring the week's total to 40.

□ In Seattle, Washington, Local 6 of the Service Employees International Union negotiated a compressed workweek covering the City of Seattle's water pollution control plants at the request of its members, 100 plant operators. The aim was to end a rotating eight-hour-shift schedule which the members strongly disliked.

The new eight-day schedule consists of two 12-hour days followed by two 12-hour nights, and then four days off. This results in an average workweek of 42 hours, with 48 hours one week and 36 the next. Overtime problems are presented because of the Fair Labor Standards Act, and because the old contract called for an eight-hour day. The new contract defines daily overtime as hours exceeding 12 in a day. It also specifies that hours in excess of 40 per week are to be paid with compensatory time off, at straight time rates; this was the city's condition for accepting the new shift rota.

A number of continuous-process oil and chemical plants, which have adopted rotas based on 12-hour shifts, pay overtime for hours exceeding eight in a day or 40 in a week, but they reduce base rates to make average weekly earnings come out the same as before. However, when managers order genuine overtime (i.e., in excess of the agreed shift length), they compensate for the lower base rate by paying more than time and one-half.

The federal government's Alternative Work Schedules experimental program, initiated in 1979, also contains workable formulas. The program provides for experiments with six variants of flexible or gliding schedules and three variants of the compressed workweek.

All the flexible options include credit and debit hours. Credit hours are defined as any hours within the flexible schedule, but in excess of the basic work requirement, which the employee *elects* to work for his or her own purposes of varying the length of the workweek or workday. Overtime hours, on the other hand, are those in excess of eight in a day or 40 in a week which are *officially ordered in advance.*

The compressed workweek options are of four ten-hour days per week, or three 13-hour, 20-minute days per week, or nine nine-hour days spread over a two-week period. Overtime is defined as hours in excess of the compressed schedule for full-time employees. For example, if the schedule calls for four ten-hour days in a week, overtime is paid only for work performed outside the schedule, i.e., in excess of ten hours in a day or 40 hours in a week.

Thus far, the experiments have done no harm to either the statutes or the unions. The question for the 1980s is how to enjoy greater flexibility without endangering the rights of employees, unionized or not. When a union waives the protection of the statutes, the act can be said to be voluntary, but in the absence of a union, who can say?

recommendation
49

Congress should not amend the overtime laws until a formula is found which does not expose workers to exploitation. When a union local wants the compressed workweek, or flexitime with debits and credits, the laws are not an insuperable bar. True, if they were more elastic, employers would find it easier to institute new work schedules unilaterally. However, new work schedules are most effective and durable when adopted by agreement between employer and employees.

recommendation
50

International unions should open discussions with their locals regarding new work schedules and should suggest how individual workers' needs and objections can be met.

NOTES

1. U.S. Bureau of Labor Statistics, "Ten Million Americans Work Flexible Schedules, 2 Million Work Full Time in Three to Four-and-a-Half Days." News release, U.S. Department of Labor, Office of Information, Washington, D.C., February 24, 1981.

2. Stanley Nollen and Virginia Hider Martin, *Alternative Work Schedules* (New York: AMACOM, a division of the American Management Associations, 1978).

3. U. S. Bureau of Labor Statistics, "Ten Million Americans Work . . ." News release, February 24, 1981.